# MANHATTAN

# URBAN NAVIGATOR

## IRA SALTZ

Little, Brown and Company

Boston   Toronto   London

**To Deri, whose mind and hands
were invaluable in shaping this book.**

First Edition

ISBN 0-316-76974-6

10 9 8 7 6 5 4 3 2 1

Published simultaneously in Canada by Little, Brown & Company
(Canada) Limited

Printed in the United States of America

Down the block from one of New York's most highly regarded restaurants (Gotham Bar and Grill) is a store that is crammed with the books, magazines, and detritus of science fiction (Forbidden Planet). Two blocks from the fashion outpost of Saks Fifth Avenue, you can eat crisp blintzes and sour cream on the mezzanine floor of 4 West 47th Street overlooking the cluttered stalls of the diamond bazaar (Diamond Dairy Restaurant). On a blazing summer day head toward the grandeur of landmark Grand Central Terminal, where, descending into the cool depths beneath New York's most imposing architectural space, you can lunch on the city's foremost array of briny oysters and seafood (Oyster Bar). Emerging refreshed, cross the street and experience the aesthetic pleasures of the Whitney Museum Annex at the Philip Morris building. Then proceed west to the TKTS booth at Times Square, where you will find theater tickets for many of the evening's performances at half price. Or after viewing a performance art piece in Tribeca (Franklin Furnace), contemplate its implications down the block at one of downtown's trendsetting restaurants (Robert De Niro's Tribeca Grill) where gustatory pleasures are enhanced by the opportunity to observe the creative world's glitterati. Then time-travel through the blue haze of the nearby Wetlands Club, where groups like Dread Zeppelin bring back the 1960s. And finally, in Manhattan's predawn stillness, amble south down Broadway to Battery Park and watch the sun rise over New York Harbor from the Staten Island Ferry.

The disparate and unexpected juxtapositions of unique and legendary restaurants, eclectic shops and boutiques, world-renowned museums, landmark architecture, glittering theater, and pulsating nightlife create the cultural dynamic of Manhattan. The *Urban Navigator* is a tool for exploring the best of these resources through a series of maps (NavigatorMaps) with keyed listings and associated symbols that locate and describe individual city highlights. Look at a NavigatorMap; see where you are or plan to be; and all the most interesting offerings of the city that surround you become accessible. By showing what's around the corner or a block away, the Navigator reveals both the exotic and the indigenous and encourages the serendipitous discovery that is often the most memorable part of a travel experience.

This guide is designed for both first-time visitors and native New Yorkers. With a business meeting downtown on Maiden Lane, a midtown advertising executive can see at a glance the closest subway stop and an array of nearby restaurants. An out-of-towner going to the Metropolitan Museum of Art, referring to the guide, will see the designer shops on nearby Madison Avenue, a lunch spot, the location of a subway back to the hotel, a restaurant convenient to the theater for dinner, and a choice of piano bars for a nightcap. All this information is organized visually in a format that reflects the way a complex urban environment is actually seen and explored.

Geographically, and often culturally, New York is defined by its neighborhoods, and their boundaries form the organizational structure of the guide. Detailed NavigatorMaps integrate the city's resources area by area. Each street map features subway routes and station locations, restaurants (with price range, type of cuisine, and, often, other descriptive symbols), shopping options (from major department stores to one-of-a-kind specialty shops), Broadway and Off-Broadway theaters, historic buildings (with architect and date of completion), museums, art galleries, and nightlife venues.

Nine easy-to-read NavigatorMaps include more than 750 locations and listings, comprising what is probably the greatest concentration of resources within any city in the world. Arranged sequentially from the Battery at the southern tip of Manhattan and moving north, they include:

## NavigatorMap 1
Battery to Canal Street.

Historic Battery Park, terminals for the Staten Island and Statue of Liberty ferries, the **Financial District** (Wall Street), the World Trade Center, the new World Financial Center, and Battery Park City fill the lower tip of Manhattan. Further north are City Hall, the heart of **Chinatown**, and **Tribeca** (TRIangle BElow CAnal), an area in transition from food distribution warehouses and industrial lofts to upscale high-rise housing, hip restaurants, and artists' lofts.

## NavigatorMap 2
Canal Street to Houston Street.

In **Little Italy**, pasta and pastry are rapidly losing ground to bok choy and barbecued duck from a sprawling **Chinatown** that is inching its way north from Canal Street. Mulberry Street with its sidewalk cafés and checkered-tablecloth restaurants is the main commercial strip. **Soho** (SOuth of HOuston), set amid many of the city's landmark nineteenth-century cast-iron buildings, is the home of the downtown art scene, with West Broadway and its environs providing fashionable "see and be seen" gallery browsing, shopping (window or otherwise), and dining.

## NavigatorMap 3
Houston Street to 14th Street.

With Washington Square its spiritual center, **Greenwich Village** pulsates with an eclectic mix of Off-Broadway theaters, bars for every taste and sexual orientation, nightclubs with the city's best jazz, small informal restaurants, relaxed coffeehouses (listed under nightspots), streetwise fashion shopping, and New York University. West of Sixth Avenue are the quiet, twisting streets of an earlier New York, the **West Village**, with a large gay population. The **East Village**, east of Third Avenue, is an enclave of old ethnic communities, punk rockers, fringe political groups, and the aspiringly creative.

## NavigatorMap 4
14th Street to 28th Street.

**Chelsea**, west of Fifth Avenue, mixes light-industrial and residential blocks, restaurants, dance theaters, small shops, and the expansive outpost of men's (and recently women's) fashion, Barney's. Union Square Park hosts a farmer's market on Wednesday, Friday, and Saturday, and the wholesale flower and plant market is on Sixth Avenue in the upper 20s. Fifth Avenue south of the Flatiron Building on 23rd Street (the **Flatiron District**) is a developing shopping corridor of youthful high fashion. To the east is the residential area of Gramercy Park, with access to the park by key to residents only.

## NavigatorMap 5
28th Street to 41st Street

Showrooms, factories, and racks of garments moved by hand and truck crowd the **Garment District**, west of Fifth Avenue. Bisecting the congestion is the aggressive retailing of 34th Street, dominated by Macy's at Seventh Avenue and nearby A&S. The Empire State Building is at Fifth Avenue, which forms the border of residential **Murray Hill** to the east. The Jacob Javits Convention Center extends from 34th to 39th Streets along Eleventh Avenue.

## NavigatorMap 6
41st Street to 50th Street.

The **Theater District**, the glare of Times Square, and the glitter of the **Diamond District** (47th Street between Sixth and Seventh Avenues) contrast with the corporate reserve of **Rockefeller Center**. To the east of Fifth Avenue is Grand Central Terminal, whose rescue from the wrecker's ball sparked the architectural preservation movement in New York, and along the East River is the **United Nations** complex.

## NavigatorMap 7
50th Street to 60th Street.

The heart of **midtown** and site of corporate America'a most prestigious office towers, including the Seagram Building, the AT&T building, and CBS headquarters ("Black Rock"). The Museum of Modern Art, The Plaza Hotel, Bloomingdale's, and many of Manhattan's most expensive restaurants provide additional cachet. From Third Avenue to Carnegie Hall, opulent **57th Street** is home to international designer fashions, prominent art galleries, and the jewels of Tiffany.

## NavigatorMap 8
60th Street to 74th Street.

On the **Upper West Side**, Lincoln Center, new anonymous residential high rises, and the upwardly mobile shopping and dining of **Columbus Avenue** border **Central Park**. Planned by Olmsted and Vaux in 1858, the greenery of the Park provides a recreational oasis for millions of nature-starved New Yorkers. To the east is the more traditionally affluent **Upper East Side**, where other new anonymous residential towers coexist with embassies, townhouses, **Madison Avenue**'s expensive shops, and the city's most exclusive co-ops on Park and Fifth Avenues.

## NavigatorMap 9
74th Street to 88th Street

The core of the **Upper West Side** has many architecturally rich prewar apartment buildings, more high-style shopping and dining on **Columbus Avenue**, melting-pot dynamics on Broadway, and the Museum of Natural History. On the **Upper East Side**'s Fifth Avenue high culture is on display at the Metropolitan Museum of Art, the Guggenheim, Cooper-Hewitt, Frick and others.

*Though the Upper East and Upper West Sides are ususally experienced separately, to maintain consistent orientation NavigatorMaps 8 and 9 show both.*

## USING THE GUIDE

The NavigatorMaps and simple graphic symbols are designed for quick reference and ease of use. Each category— restaurants, shops, landmarks, museums and galleries, theaters, and nightlife—is represented by a color-coded symbol. Numbers on the maps, in matching colors, correspond to the full numbered listing on the facing page. Many of the written listings use symbols to convey additional information. The inside back cover describes all symbols and abbreviations used throughout the book and also provides a list of useful telephone numbers.

If you know the name of a destination but not its location, use the index at the back of the book. The alphabetized entries are shown with references to the NavigatorMap on which they can be found and their number on that map. There is a neighborhood key to the nine NavigatorMaps on page 36.

Telephone numbers are given for listings; it is always advisable to call ahead to check opening and closing times. Museums may be closed one day of the week, some stores may be open Sunday but not Saturday, and there are restaurants that are open only for dinner. At all but the least expensive restaurants, call to see if reservations are necessary.

## GETTING AROUND

While subway and bus routes crisscross the city, the best way to get the feel of the city is on foot. It is also the quickest way to go a short distance in midtown during business hours. A story about two New Yorkers overheard on a street corner makes the point: "Shall we walk," one said to the other, "or do we have time to take a cab?" If you choose to walk, beware of New York's daredevil bicycle messengers, who frequently ignore both traffic signals and one-way streets.

For covering longer distances like midtown to Wall Street, the most efficient transportation is the **subway**, and, if you are not conspicuous in your affluence, it is safer than the tabloids would have you believe. The megamillionaire Hunt Brothers and Adnan Khashoggi have been caught using the subway. There is safety in numbers, however, and late at night, when the subways are fairly deserted, would be a judicious time to take a cab. Subways require a token, available from token booths at subway stations. The fare is the same for one stop or to the end of the line.

**Buses** are cleaner, quieter, and less forbidding, but usually much slower, particularly during business hours. Exact change (no dollar bills) or a subway token is required. North of 14th Street, buses operate on all north/south avenues from York Avenue to Tenth Avenue, except Park Avenue. Streets with east/west crosstown buses are indicated on NavigatorMaps with the bus symbol. Bus symbols shown on two consecutive streets indicate one-way streets, with even- numbered streets running east. South of 14th Street, many major avenues and streets have bus routes. Bus stops, often at glass-enclosed shelters, are well marked, and specific route information and approximate schedules are posted.

For bus transportation to or from the **airports**, call Carey (1-718-632-0500) for specific pick-up information and departure times, Olympia Trails (964-6233), operating from the World Trade Center only, or New Jersey Transit (1-201-762-5100), to Newark Airport only.

**Taxis**, licensed by the city and painted bright yellow, are available if the numbered rooftop light is on. If the adjacent off-duty lights are also on, the cab will probably not pick you up unless your destination coincides with the driver's. Only licensed yellow cabs are allowed to cruise for passengers. For reasons that are clear only to the cab industry, many taxicabs are "off-duty" during rush hour. In bad weather or rush hour, 8:00 to 9:00 A.M. and 5:00 to 6:00 P.M., it is nearly impossible to find a vacant cab. If you are lucky enough to spot one under these conditions, be aggressive in securing it, or an umbrella-wielding little old lady in sneakers may appear out of nowhere to usurp your prize. Some cab drivers don't know their way around the city or have limited knowledge of English; a NavigatorMap will be useful in communicating your destination.

**Car and limousine services** are useful for a prearranged pick-up, to get to the airport, or in the outlying areas of the city where yellow cabs do not cruise for passengers. Carmel (662-2222), Tel-Aviv (505-0555), and Vista (777-4600) are among many listed in the Yellow Pages telephone directory. Always determine rates in advance; they are based on destination and/or travel time and the luxuriousness of the vehicle.

On temperate weekends when traffic is less hazardous, **bicycles** are not an unreasonable way to explore the city, particularly Central Park. Bicycles can be rented at Metro Bicycle Stores (255-5100), Pedal Pusher (288-5592), and other bicycle stores listed in the Yellow Pages. Beware. Unattended bicycles are vulnerable to theft, even when locked up. (The leading manufacturer of hardened steel "theft-proof" locks guarantees its locks everywhere–but New York City.)

And finally, **driving** in Manhattan is a slow, harrowing, and expensive proposition, especially during business hours. Legal street parking is virtually nonexistent (illegally parked cars are often towed), and there is a 14% city tax on already very expensive garage rates.

## PLEASURES/AMENITIES

For many New Yorkers, brown bagging and sunlight are a perfect combination for the ideal lunch. Join them at vest-pocket parks (Paley Park on 53rd Street east of Fifth Avenue is an architectural jewel), glass-enclosed atriums (the Winter Garden at the World Financial Center, and the street-level courtyard of the IBM building on 57th Street stand out), expansive building plazas

(Chase Manhattan Plaza in the Financial District and the Seagram Building on East 53rd Street), and, of course, public parks. All are free and open to the public, and some offer a limited variety of sandwiches and snacks or are near delicatessens with sandwich and salad bars. Street vendors also proliferate throughout the city and their wares represent an international variety of foods.

Public **restrooms** are difficult to find. Plan ahead. Department stores, museums, the better hotels, and restaurants (if you are a patron or look respectable) are your best bet. Also many office buildings with atriums and plazas, such as Citicorp Center, the Whitney Museum at Philip Morris, the IBM Building, and Trump Tower, have restrooms open to the public.

During the spring and summer there are free concerts, opera, and Shakespeare in the parks. Check the *New York Times* for details, or call this special event number: 360-1333.

## RESTAURANTS

One of the criteria for selecting restaurants to be featured in this guide is a correlation between how much you pay for a meal and the quality of the food. If the food is superior to the cost, often a result of less contrived or nonexistent atmosphere, more casual service, or marginal location, the listing will include a chef's hat with a plus sign. Factors such as atmosphere, trendiness, and music, represented by symbols, may also explain a restaurant's being listed. The coffee-mug symbol designates a neighborhood favorite, and the big apple star is awarded to establishments that are uniquely "New York" with outstanding reputations.

Restaurants in as wide a price range as possible have been included in the guide; however, location will often dictate economics. Virtually all restaurants in the 50s will be expensive, while bargains are easily found in Chinatown and the East Village.

While many of the more expensive midtown restaurants require men to wear a jacket and tie, south of 14th Street (excluding the Financial District) the rules change. An entrepreneur of this "downtown" scene recently characterized his successful restaurants as dependent on "a group of 200 beautiful people dressed in black."

Again, always call to see if reservations are taken. At the trendiest and most fashionable restaurants, where gaining admission is an achievement, it may be necessary to make reservations weeks in advance and, after arriving at the appointed hour, to endure an extended wait at the bar. Consider whether or not it is worth the effort to catch a glimpse of Bianca or Calvin.

However, with less money being lavished on expensive meals lately, some of Manhattan's costlier restaurants are lowering prices and developing simpler menus. Pretension and attitude levels are dropping. You are less likely to encounter the kind of reply one New Yorker received at one of the city's pricier lunch spots when he asked the waiter what came with the very expensive Dover sole. The waiter's unequivocal response: "A plate and the check."

## SHOPPING

There is probably no other place with as great a diversity of things to buy as New York. Virtually every designer label or brand is available here. From renowned department stores like Macy's and Bloomingdale's to the narrowly focused shops that specialize in single product categories like wind-up toys (The Last Wound-Up), light bulbs (Just Bulbs), music boxes (Rita Ford), or largescale replicas (Think Big), New York has it for sale. The NavigatorMaps and listings include both the world-famous emporiums and many of the smaller eclectic shops that have earned reputations for quality, style, low prices, or unique products.

Often neighborhoods offer clusters of stores with similar fashion points of view or attract a particular type of customer.

Within a one-block radius of **Madison Avenue and 45th Street** you'll find Paul Stuart, Brooks Brothers, Tripler, Chipp, and J. Press, long-established men's stores catering to the conservative and fashionably understated.

In **Soho**, where ponytails are considered more stylish on men than women, the more aggressively fashionable stores provide accoutrements for the all-black "downtown" look, as well as the wares of leading-edge European and Japanese designers. Wandering some of the cobblestoned streets, you can discover fashion outposts like Comme des Garcons and Diane Benson, high-style houseware and furnishing shops like Zona and D. F. Sanders, and the consumate purveyors of the edible, Dean and Deluca, where observing the food is almost as satisfying as eating it.

**Columbus Avenue** on the Upper West Side presents a range of upscale urban fashions for the young professionals of the area. In addition to stores like Charivari for "statement fashions," the toy store for adults, Mythology, and the epicurian shrine of Zabar's provide other pleasures.

**Lower Fifth Avenue** from 14th to 23rd Streets, the Flatiron District, is developing a reputation for designer sportswear and accessories from shops like Emporio Armani and Paul Smith, exotic eyeglasses from Alan Mikli, and discounted fashions at Daffy's, all within range of Barney's on Seventh Avenue.

**Greenwich Village** generally attracts a younger, funkier clientele with its lower-priced merchandise. It also has a profusion of shops with used or antique clothing (Unique), used books (Strand Book Store), and used records (Bleeker Bob's).

On the outskirts of the congestion and noise of midtown Manhattan, the **South Street Seaport** and **World Financial Center** have many small fashionable shops and outlets of major stores in an atmosphere not unlike an upscale suburban shopping mall.

And on **Madison Avenue** in the 60s and 70s, where shopping and strolling are compatible, you'll see the designer-clothing boutiques and hair salons where affluent and fashionable New Yorkers acquire their panache.

Cartier, Gucci, Rolex, Louis Vuitton, and Ralph Lauren are sold in the city's most exclusive shops on upper Fifth and Madison Avenues. Spend a Saturday threading your way through the throngs on **Canal Street** and you'll find it difficult to avoid stepping on products with these same prestigious logos arrayed on the sidewalk. But if you're tempted by a $25.00 "gold Rolex," you also won't want to pass up the great buy from the fellow selling the Brooklyn Bridge.

Shop carefully and you can find **excellent values** in New York. The enormous volume of merchandise that passes through the city virtually guarantees that someone somewhere is selling what you want at markdown prices. Many of the major department stores have some discounted merchandise throughout the year, and storewide clearances in early summer and after Christmas are common in even the most exclusive shops. Cameras and electronics can be found heavily discounted (Forty Seventh Street Photo, Executive Photo, E-33, Uncle Steve), but shop carefully, getting prices on comparable models and warranty information. Some discounted name brand products will not be serviced by the American distributor if they have been imported (even legally) through alternate channels.

Many, but not all, retail stores are open Sunday. Many of the discount camera and electronic stores are owned and operated by orthodox Jews and close from sundown on Friday through Saturday. Weekends there are a number of excellent **flea markets** with unique, inexpensive clothing and jewelry (Tower flea market on Broadway between 4th Street and Great Jones, I.S. 44 flea market on Columbus Avenue and 76th Street, Sunday only, and the Spring Street flea market on Spring and Wooster Streets, open daily), as well as a proliferation of street vendors (Broadway, south of 8th Street, Canal Street, and scattered throughout the city).

## THEATER/CONCERTS

From mimes and jugglers performing for a sidewalk audience for small change to lavishly produced Broadway shows where $50 seats are reserved months in advance, there are concerts and theater in New York for all tastes and budgets. There is dance theater in Chelsea (the Joyce and Dance Theater Workshop), the Metropolitan Opera and New York Philharmonic at Lincoln Center, Off-Broadway theater (less expensive and more adventuresome than Broadway) on West 42nd Street, Greenwich Village and other locations, and Off-Off-Broadway theater (where modest admission prices or voluntary contributions fuel highly experimental and often fleeting vignettes of dramatic aspiration) in the more remote reaches of downtown lofts, basements, and churches. Look for reviews of major Broadway and Off-Broadway productions in the *New York Times*. The *New Yorker* and *New York* magazines provide both current reviews and capsule summaries of past reviews for many ongoing productions. The best source of information for the more peripheral Off-Broadway and Off-Off-Broadway productions is the weekly *Village Voice*. Street performers (particularly on weekends in the warmer months) can usually be found at Washington Square Park, the Metropolitan Museum of Art entrance steps, and the 60th Street and Fifth Avenue entrance to Central Park.

Theater and concert tickets are available at theater box offices, where you can see the exact location of your seat, and by phone from Ticketron (399-4444), which adds a service charge and also has locations throughout Manhattan. Half-price theater tickets are available the day of performance from TKTS in Times Square at 47th Street, 3:00 to 8:00 P.M., and Number 2 World Trade Center, mezzanine, 11 to 5:30, also with a small service charge. (Telephone information for both locations: 354-5800.) Music and dance half-price tickets can be purchased the day of performance at Bryant Park, 42nd Street east of Sixth Avenue. Call after 12:30 for availability (382-2323).

## MUSEUMS/GALLERIES

Art, like fashion, can be discovered in the streets as well as the institutions of the city. Keith Haring first chalked his ubiquitous figures on blackened subway billboards. One Greenwich Village artist glues fragments of china and pottery, mosaic-like, on streetlamp bases (with the city's permission). Look for his work around Astor Place and Broadway, south of Eighth Street. Loft buildings and construction sites in Soho are often clandestinely plastered with billboards decrying the sexual inequity of the art world and signed by a group called the Guerilla Girls. Considered by some a form of artistic expression, the billboards themselves are furtively removed by would-be collectors.

The downtown galleries and small museums of Tribeca and Soho show the newest, most experimental art. The galleries on 57th Street and the area around upper Madison Avenue exhibit more established contemporary artists as well as traditional art from earlier periods. In addition, auction houses have previews of merchandise prior to sale date.

Among the city's major museums:

The **Whitney Museum of American Art**, designed by Marcel Breuer, is devoted to American artists. Its Biennial exhibit is a closely watched indicator of what's current. (Closed Monday)

The **Guggenheim Museum** with its spiraling ramp, Frank Lloyd Wright's only architectural work in New York City, is increasingly the arena for conceptual and minimalist art, while maintaining its strong position in early-20th-century abstract art, particularly Kandinsky. (Closed Monday)

The **Museum of Modern Art (MOMA)**, founded in 1929, is the progenitor of the modern art museum. Its collection spans the late 19th century through the present. In addition to painting and sculpture departments, the museum includes architecture and design, photography, and movies. Its outdoor sculpture garden, which hosts free summer concerts, provides a cloistered and serene respite from surrounding midtown. (Closed Wednesday)

The **Frick Collection** is one of the city's jewels. Converted from the mansion of Henry Clay Frick, it houses his collection of 14th- to 19th-century masterpieces. (Closed Monday)

Medieval armor or Greek vases, the Egyptian temple of Dendur or dugout canoes from New Guinea, Rembrandt and Velasquez or Picasso—the **Metropolitan Museum of Art** is extraordinary in the depth and range of its collections. As with other museums in the city, weekdays are far less crowded than weekends. (Closed Monday)

The **American Museum of Natural History** maintains an encyclopedic collection of over 34 million specimens and objects representing the world's flora and fauna, including mammoth dinosaur skeletons, a full-size 90-foot-long whale replica, and the Star of India sapphire.

A number of museums that normally charge admission have hours when entrance is free or payment voluntary. Call individual museums for details of their fee policy.

## LANDMARKS

Though much of Manhattan's historic past has been obliterated by waves of development, there are a few remaining vestiges of the original Dutch or Colonial settlements at the southern tip of Manhattan. **St. Paul's Chapel** (1764) still stands, and **Trinity Church**, erected in 1681 and rebuilt in its present form in 1846, provides a striking focal point when viewed from the canyon of Wall Street.

The city, now increasingly aware of the loss of its distant heritage, the brazen destruction of its recent past (Pennsylvania Station), and continuing attempts to desecrate existing buildings (Grand Central Terminal), has been conferring landmark status on buildings erected as recently as 30 years ago (**Lever House**, the **Seagram Building**). But for preservationists, what remains the city's most sacred ground is some 800 acres of what was originally swamp land, hog farms, and rock ledges. Designed by Frederick Law Olmsted and Calvert Vaux in 1858, **Central Park** continues to flourish as a refuge from the hard edges of the city. There is a recently refurbished zoo (861-6030), running, bicycling, and horseback riding paths, the Wollman ice-skating rink (517-4800), and a program of summer cultural activities (360-1333).

For many, the symbol of Manhattan is its awe-inspiring skyline, a view of untrammeled vertical growth that contrasts with the orderliness of its numbered street grid (established in 1811 for the area north of 14th Street). The buildings that define the skyline chronicle the evolution of modern architecture: The **Flatiron Building** (1902) was one of the earliest steel-skeleton structures; the **Woolworth Building** (1913) was the world's tallest until completion of the art nouveau **Chrysler Building** (1930), which was quickly eclipsed by the **Empire State Building** (1931). The International style **Lever House** (1952) and **Seagram Building** (1958) set the tone for the metal- and glass-walled building boom that followed. The 110-story twin towers of the **World Trade Center** (1962-1977) now dominate the lower Manhattan skyline with their bulk if not their artistry.

## VIEWS

Ferries leaving from Battery Park (built, like much of the southern tip of Manhattan, from landfill), for the **Statue of Liberty**, **Ellis Island**, and **Staten Island** cross Upper New York Bay, offering some of the most dramatic views of the lower Manhattan skyline. (There can be long lines for the Ellis Island ferry; call 269-5755 for timely departure information.) For a trip around the island of Manhattan, the **Circle Line** (563-3200) leaves from 42nd Street at the Hudson River and is an excellent introduction to the city.

For bird's-eye views of the city, the **Empire State Building** (736-3100) and the **World Trade Center** (466-7397) have observation decks.

## NIGHTLIFE

Woody Allen captured the range of New York night life in *Hannah and Her Sisters* with his scenes of a date that started downtown at the heavy metal rock club CBGB's and ended uptown at the Carlyle Hotel listening to Bobby Short vocalize old standards at the piano. Uptown is older and more establishment; downtown (below 14th Street) more diverse and casual (wear all black and you'll probably be mistaken for a native).

Greenwich Village and Soho, downtown, offer long-established bars where you can have a relaxed drink and get a sense of the area's character (the Lion's Head — a literary hangout, Fanelli — artists and dealers), coffeehouses rich in tradition (Caffe Dante, Caffe Reggio), clubs for listening to music (the Bottom Line — mostly rock and folk, the Blue Note — jazz), and dance clubs (Nell's, S.O.B.'s). Check the *Village Voice* for current attractions and admission policies at the clubs. If you want to glimpse the cutting edge of New York nightlife, *Interview* magazine tracks the quicksilver comings and goings of the phenomena.

## PLAYING IT SAFE

Exercising the good judgement that for many New Yorkers is second nature can help ensure a safe visit. Avoid flaunting jewelry or cash, don't leave possessions unattended (like suitcases at a hotel entrance), and if you have a car, keep it in an attended garage. Purses should be securely closed and are best kept in laps rather than slung over the back of a restaurant chair. Yellow cabs are the safest way around the city at night. And finally, enjoy Manhattan with the confidence of a native; don't wander the streets like a lost lamb, gazing apprehensively at passersby as if everyone were a potential  mugger.

## A FINAL WORD

The format of the *Urban Navigator*, designed to make the best of Manhattan easily accessible to visitors and natives, must inevitably omit some personal favorites. Displaying the texture of an area as well as offering diversity means balancing factors such as location, uniqueness, price, historical significance, style, and reputation. Additionally, shops, restaurants, and nightspots are constantly opening, closing and reinventing themselves. Every attempt has been made to be current and accurate, and we regret any errors that may occur. We hope you will let us know your impressions, both good and bad, and any suggestions for new entries.

The area included in the *Urban Navigator* contains the multiplicity of attractions that are a focal point for many visitors and New Yorkers. Beyond the boundaries of this book, upper Manhattan and the city's other boroughs offer visitors their own special rewards. You might want to sample Sylvia's, a Harlem institution for southern soul food at 328 Lenox Avenue at West 127th Street (966-0660); Peter Luger's, perhaps *the* classic New York steak house, across the Williamsburg Bridge in Brooklyn at 178 Broadway (1-718-387-7400); Brooklyn Heights, along the East River from the Brooklyn Bridge to Atlantic Avenue, a vestige of the 19th century with spectacular esplanade views of lower Manhattan; and the Bronx Zoo, with natural habitats for many of its 3500 animals (367-1010).

**🍴**

1 **Au Mandarin** *Ch* $$$ ❂
250 Vesey, 385-0310

2 **Donald Sacks** *Am* $ ❂
250 Vesey, 619-4600

3 **Cellar in the Sky** *Am* $$$$ ❂
1 World Trade Ctr., 938-1111

4 **Windows on World Hors d'Oeuvrerie** *Cont* $$ ❂
Windows/World *Cont* $$$$ ❂ ❂ ❂
1 World Trade Center, 938-1111

5 **American Harvest** *Cont*
3 World Trade Ctr., 432-9334

6 **Delmonico's** *Am ST* $$$
56 Beaver, 422-4747

7 **La Barca** *It*
40 Fletcher, 514-9704

8 **Sweets** *Am SF* $$$
2 Fulton, 825-9786

9 **Harbour Lights** *Am* $$ ❂
Fulton/South, 227-2800

10 **Ponte's** *It* $$$
39 Debrosses, 226-4621

11 **Capsouto Freres** *Fr* $$$ ❂
451 Washington, 966-4900

12 **Thai House Cafe** *Th* $$ X ⊕
151 Hudson, 334-1085

13 **Tribeca Grill** *Am* $$$ ↩
375 Greenwich, 941-3900

14 **Chanterelle** *Fr* $$$$ ❂
2 Harrison, 966-6960

15 **Tommy Tang's** *Th*
323 Greenwich, 334-9190

16 **Bouley** *Fr* $$$ ❂ ❂
165 Duane, 608-3852

17 **Hamburger Harry's** *Am* $
157 Chambers, 267-4446

18 **Il Giglio** *It*
81 Warren, 571-5555

19 **Duane Park Cafe** *Am/Ec* $$$
157 Duane, 732-5555

20 **One Hudson Cafe** *Cont*
1 Hudson, 608-5835

21 **Montrachet** *Fr* $$$$
239 W. Broadway, 219-2777

22 **El Teddy's** *Mx* $$ ↩
219 W. Broadway, 941-7070

23 **Odeon** *Fr* $$
145 W. Broadway, 233-0507

24 **Rosemarie's** *It*
145 Duane, 285-2610

25 **Le Zinc** *Fr* $$$ ↩
139 Duane, 732-1226

26 **Ecco** *It* $$$
124 Chambers, 227-7074

27 **Barocco** *It* $$$ ↩
301 Church, 431-1445

28 **Arqua** *It* $$$ ↩
281 Church, 334-1888

29 **Thailand Restaurant** *Th* $ ⊕
106 Bayard, 349-3132

30 **Big Wong** *Ch* $ ⊕ 🔒
67 Mott, 964-0540

31 **Mandarin Court** *Ch* $
61 Mott, 608-3838

32 **Bo Ky** *Ch/Vi* $ X 🔒
80 Bayard, 406-2292

33 **Tai Hong Lau** *Ch* $$ X
70 Mott, 219-1431

34 **Wonton Garden** *Ch* $ ↩ ⊕
56 Mott, 966-4886

35 **Oriental Town** *Ch.SF* $$ X ⊕ 🔒
14 Elizabeth, 619-0085

36 **King Fung** *Ch* $
20 Elizabeth, 964-5256

37 **20 Mott Street** *Ch* $$
20 Mott, 964-0380

38 **Phoenix Garden** *Ch* $$ X
46 Bowery, 962-8934

39 **Bridge Cafe** *Am* $$ ❣ 🔒
279 Water, 227-3344

40 **Golden Unicorn** *Ch* $$
18 E. Broadway, 941-0911

41 **Great Shanghai** *Ch* $ ⊕
27 Division, 966-7663

42 **Canton** *Ch* $$ X
45 Division, 226-4441

43 **Hwa Yuan Szechuan** *Ch* $ ⊕
40 E. Broadway, 966-5534

44 **Nice Restaurant** *Ch* $$
35 E. Broadway, 406-9510

**🛍️**

1 **Syms** % 797-1199
42 Trinity Pl *M Clothing*

2 **Century 21** % 227-9092
22 Cortlandt *Clothing*

3 **Job Lot Trading** % 962-4142
140 Church *Housewares*

4 **Pearl Paint** 431-7932
308 Canal *Art Supplies*

5 **Tents & Trails** 227-1760
21 Park Pl *Outdoor Equipment*

**🌙**

1 **Caroline's** 233-4900
89 South St *Comedy Club*

2 **Wetlands** ♫ 966-4225
161 Hudson *Hippie Rock*

3 **North River Bar** ♫ 226-9411
145 Hudson *Rock/Roll Dancing*

4 **Riverrun Cafe** 🄿 966-3894
176 Franklin *Bar*

5 **Puffy's Tavern** 🄿 ❂ 766-9159
81 Hudson *Bar*

6 **Katie O'Toole's** 226-9268
134 Reade *Bar*

7 **McGovern's Bar** 227-2295
135 Reade *Bar*

8 **Exodus** 274-1915
21 Hudson *Dancing*

9 **Nancy Whiskey Pub** 226-9943
1 Lispenard *Bar*

10 **Raccoon Lodge** 🄿 766-9656
59 Warren *Bar*

11 **Jeremy's Ale House** 964-3537
259 Front *Bar*

**🏛️**

1 **World Financial Center**
Vesey/West St *Pelli*

2 **Battery Park City** ❂ 1979
West St/Battery-Chambers St

3 **World Trade Center** ❂ 1962-77
Church/Vesey *Yamasaki*

4 **St. Paul's Chapel** 1764
Broadway/Fulton *McBean*

5 **Trinity Church** 1681-1846
Broadway/Wall *Upjohn*

6 **Statue of Liberty** ❂ (Ferry)
Battery Park

7 **Ellis Island** (Ferry)
Battery Park

8 **N.Y. Stock Exchange** 1903
8 Broad *Post*

9 **U.S. Customs House** 1907
Whitehall/Bridge

10 **Chase Manhattan Plaza** 1960
Nassau/Liberty *Skidmore et al*

11 **40 Wall St.** 1929
40 Wall St *Severance & Matsui*

12 **Staten Island Ferry** ❂
Battery Park

13 **Fraunces Tavern** 1763
54 Pearl

14 **South St. Seaport**
South St/Fulton

15 **Woolworth Building** 1913
233 Broadway *Gilbert*

16 **City Hall** 1802-1811 B'way/
Murray *Mangin & McComb*

17 **Municipal Building** 1914
1 Centre *McKim, Mead & White*

18 **Brooklyn Bridge** ❂ 1883
Park Row/Centre *Roebling*

**🖼️**

1 **Whitney Downtown** 943-5655
33 Maiden Lane *Contemp. Art*

2 **Cavin-Morris** 226-3768
100 Hudson *Contemp. Art*

3 **Artists Space** 226-3970
223 W. Broadway, *Art, Videos*

4 **Franklin Furnace** 925-4671
112 Franklin *Performance, Books*

5 **Alternative Museum** 966-4444
17 White *Political Art*

6 **Clocktower**, 233-1096
108 Leonard *Avant-Garde Art*

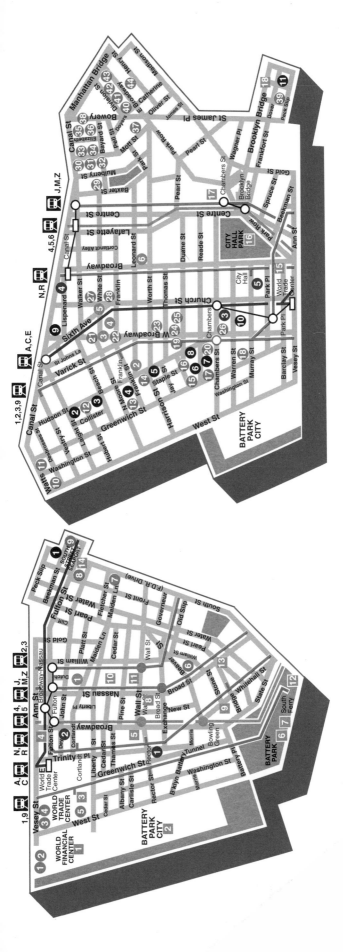

**Restaurants**

4 ... rr $$$ ☎
- 38 MacDougal, 475-7500
5 Elephant & Castle Am $ P
- 183 Prince, 260-3600
6 Raoul's Fr $$$ ✆
- 180 Prince, 966-3518
7 Omen Ja ☎
- 113 Thompson, 925-8923
8 Mezzogiorno It $$ X
- 195 Spring, 334-2112
9 Lupe's East L.A. Mx $ X
- 110 Sixth Av, 966-1326
10 Vucciria It $$$ ✆
- 422 W. Broadway, 941-5811
11 Ameci Miei It $$
- 475 W. Broadway, 533-1933
12 I Tre Merli It $$$ ✆/ ☎
- 463 W. Broadway, 254-8699
13 Tennessee Mountain Am BBQ $$
- 143 Spring, 431-3993
14 Cinco de Mayo Mx $$
- 349 W. Broadway 226-5255

15 Greene Street Cafe Am $$$ P ♪
- 101 Greene, 925-2415
16 Manhattan Bistro Fr $$
- 129 Spring, 966-3459
17 Jerry's Am/Ec $ ✆
- 101 Prince, 966-9464
18 Amsterdam's Am $$ ✆
- 454 Broadway, 925-6166
19 Lulu's It $$$
- 430 Broome, 925-5858
20 Pietro & Vanessa It $$
- 23 Cleveland, 941-0286
21 Grotta Azzurra It $$$ X
- 387 Broome, 925-8775
22 Taormina It $$$
- 147 Mulberry, 219-1007
23 S.P.Q.R. It $$$
- 133 Mulberry, 925-3120
24 Il Cortile It $$$ ☎
- 125 Mulberry, 226-6060
25 Ballato It $$$ X
- 55 E. Houston, 226-9683
26 Oriental Pearl Ch $$ P
- 103 Mott, 219-8388
27 Sammy's Roumanian Rm/Jw $$
- 157 Chrystie, 673-0330
28 Katz's Deli Jw $ X P
- 205 East Houston, 254-2246
29 Ratner's Dairy $ X
- 138 Delancey, 677-5588

**▢ Shopping**

1 Betsy Johnson 420-0169
- 130 Thompson W.Clothing
2 Harriet Love 966-2280
- 412 W. B'way Ant.W.Clothing
3 Spring Street Books 219-3033
- 169 Spring Books
4 Untitled 982-2088
- 159 Prince Postcards
5 Ad Hoc Softwares 925-2652
- 410 W. Broadway Designware
6 Il Bisonte 966-8773
- 72 Thompson Ital. Leathergoods
7 Think Big 925-7300
- 390 W. B'way Oversized Objects
8 D.F. Sanders ♦ 925-9040
- 386 W. Broadway Designware
9 Parachute 925-8630
- 121 Wooster Clothing
10 Knoll 925-6500
- 105 Wooster Modern Furniture
11 Putamayo 966-4458
- 147 Spring W.Clothing
12 Spring Street Flea Mkt.
- Spring & Wooster Daily 10-6
13 Tootsi Plohound 925-6641
- 124 Prince Shoes
14 Agnes B. 925-4649
- 116 Prince Clothing

15 Comme des Garcons 219-0660
- 116 Wooster Avant-Garde Clothing
16 Diane B. 219-9760
- 102 Wooster Clothing
17 Zona ☎ 925-6750
- 97 Greene Designware
18 Uncle Steve ✆ 226-4010
- 343 Canal Electronics
19 Wolfman Gold 431-1888
- 116 Greene Tableware
20 Photographers Place 431-9358
- 133 Mercer Photo Books
21 Canal Rubber 226-7339
- 329 Canal Tubing, Foam, Mats
22 Cockpit 925-5455
- 595 Broadway Aviator Gear
23 Dean & Deluca ♦ 431-1691
- 560 Broadway Gourmet Food
24 B'way Panhandler 966-3434
- 520 Broadway Kitchenware
25 Canal Jean ✆ 226-1130
- 504 Broadway Clothing
26 Urban Archeology ☎ 431-6969
- 285 Lafayette Architectural Ant.
27 Ferrara 226-6150
- 195 Grand Italian Pastry
28 Thunder & Light 219-0180
- 171 Bowery Contemp. Lighting
29 Fine & Klein ✆ 674-6720
- 119 Orchard Handbags

30 Chez Aby ✆ 431-6135
- 77 Delancey W.Clothing
31 Breakaway ✆ 598-4455
- 88 Rivington W.Clothing

**☾ Nightlife**

1 Ear Inn ♩ 226-9060
- 326 Spring Bar
2 McGovern's Bar ♪ 627-5037
- 305 Spring Blues Bar
3 S.O.B.'s ♪ 243-4940
- 204 Varick Latin. Dancing
4 Kenn's Broome St. ♩ 925-2086
- 363 W. Broadway Bar/Restaurant
5 Fanelli ♩ ☎ 226-9412
- 94 Prince Bar
6 Knitting Factory ♪ 219-3055
- 47 E. Houston Cabaret
7 Caffe Roma 226-8413
- 385 Broome Coffeehouse

**🏛 Landmarks**

1 101 Spring Street 1870
- 101 Spring Whyte
2 Haughwout Building 1857
- 488 Broadway Gaynor
3 Puck Building 1885
- 295 Lafayette Wagner
4 Police Building 1909
- 240 Center Hoppin & Koen

**Galleries**

1 Castelli, Leo ☎ 431-5160
- 420 W. Broadway Contemp. Art
2 Sonnabend 966-6160
- 420 W. Broadway Contemp. Art
3 Witkin 925-5510
- 415 W. Broadway Photography
4 Cooper, Paula 674-0766
- 155 Wooster Contemp. Art
5 Boone, Mary 431-1818
- 417 W. Broadway Contemp. Art
6 Dia Art 925-9397
- 393 W. Broadway Contemp. Art
7 O.K. Harris 431-3600
- 383 W. Broadway Contemp. Art
8 Pace 421-3292
- 142 Greene Contemp. Art
9 Weber 966-6115
- 142 Greene Contemp. Art
10 Shafrazi, Tony 925-8732
- 163 Mercer Contemp. Art
11 Milliken 966-7800
- 98 Prince Contemp. Art
12 New Museum 219-1222
- 583 Broadway Art
13 Marcuse Pfeifer 226-2251
- 568 Broadway Photography
14 Protetch, Max 966-5454
- 560 Broadway Architect. Draws

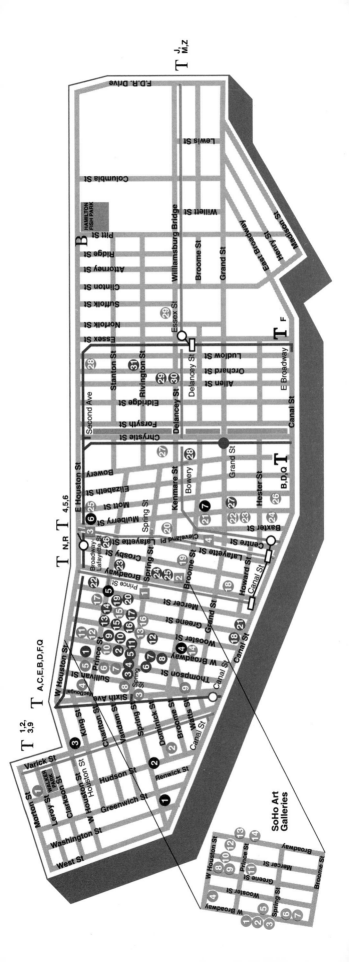

**🍴**
1 Florent *Fr* $$ ✔ — 69 Gansevoort, 989-5779
2 El Faro *Sp* $$ ⊕ — 823 Greenwich St, 929-8210
3 Cafe de la Gare *Fr* $$ ♪ — 143 Perry, 242-3553
4 La Ripaille *Fr* $$ ♥ — 605 Hudson, 255-4406
5 Jane Street Seafood *Am* $$ — 31 Eighth Ave, 243-9237
6 Corner Bistro *Am* ¢ X Y ♥ ✿ — 331 W. 4, 242-9502
7 Quatorze *Fr* $$$ ♥ — 240 W. 14, 206-7006
8 Chez Michellat *Fr* $$$ ♪ — 90 Bedford, 242-8309
9 Sevilla *Sp* $$ ♥ — 62 Charles, 929-3819
10 John Clancy's *Am SF* $$$$ — 181 W. 10, 242-7350
11 John's Pizzeria *It* ¢ X ⊕ — 278 Bleeker, 243-1680
12 Elephant & Castle *Am* $ — 68 Greenwich Ave, 243-1400
13 La Tulipe *Fr* $$$$ ♥ — 104 W. 13, 691-8860
14 Cent'Anni *It* $$ — 50 Carmine, 989-9494
15 Chez Jacqueline *Fr* $$ — 72 MacDougal, 505-0727
16 Coach House *Am* $$$ — 110 Waverly Pl, 777-0303
17 Il Mulino *It* $$$ ✿ — 86 W. 3, 673-3783
18 Portobello *It* $$ ⊕ — 208 Thompson, 473-7794
19 Arturo's *It* $ ♪ ♥ — 106 Houston, 475-9828
20 Gotham Grill *Am* $$$$ ¢ X Y ♥ ✿ — 12 E. 12, 620-4020
21 Japonica *Ja* $$ — 90 University Pl, 243-7752
22 Shima *Ja* $
23 Indochine *Vi* $$ ✔ Y — 430 Lafayette, 505-5111
24 Cucina di Pesce *It* $ X Y ⊕ — 87 E. 4, 260-6800
25 Kiev *Ru* ¢ ♥ ⊕ — 117 Second Ave, 674-4040
26 Everybody's *Fr* $$ ✔ — 31 Second Ave, 473-1884
27 Second Ave. Deli *Jw* $ X — 156 Second Ave, 677-0606
28 Veselka *Po* ¢ ♥ ⊕ — 144 Second Ave, 228-9682
29 Passage to India *In* $ ⊕ — 308 E. 6, 529-5770
30 Mitali East *In* $$ — 334 E. 6, 533-2508
31 Miracle Grill *Am* $$ X ⊕ — 112 First Ave, 254-2353
32 Tompkins Park *Am* $ — 141 Ave A, 260-4798

**🛒**
12 Tower Flea Market — 690 Broadway *Sat/Sun 11-7*
13 Astor Wine 674-7500 — 12 Astor Pl *Wine*
14 Chef Rstrnt Supply 254-6644 — 294 Bowery *Kitchenware*

**◗**
1 Gulf Coast 206-8790 — 489 West St *Tex/Mex Bar*
2 White Horse Tvrn. ✿ 243-9260 — 567 Hudson *Bar*
3 Nell's ♪ 675-1557 — 246 W. 14 *Dance Club*
4 Eighty Eights ♪ 924-0088 — 228 W. 10 *Cabaret*
5 Chumley's 675-4449 — 86 Bedford *Speakeasy/Bar*
6 Five Oaks ♪ ♥ 243-8885 — 49 Grove *Piano Bar*
7 Duplex ♪ 255-5438 — 55 Grove *Jazz*
8 Sweet Basil ♪ 242-1785 — 88 Seventh Ave S. *Jazz*
9 Village Vanguard ♪ 255-4037 — 178 Seventh Ave S. *Jazz*
10 Mostly Magic 924-1472 — 55 Carmine *Magic, Comedy*
11 Lion's Head ♥ 929-0670 — 59 Christopher *Literary Bar*
12 Fifty-Five Bar ♪ ♥ 929-9883 — 55 Christopher *Jazz*
13 Gran Caffe Artisti 255-7041 — 46 Greenwich Ave *Coffeehouse*
14 Blue Note ♪ ♥ ✿ 475-8592 — 131 W. 3 *Jazz*
15 Caffe Reggio ✿ 475-9557 — 119 MacDougal *Coffeehouse*
16 Caffe Dante 982-5275 — 79 MacDougal *Coffeehouse*
17 Village Gate ♪ 475-5120 — Bleeker & Thompson *Jazz*
18 Bradley's ♪ ♥ 228-6440 — 70 University Pl *Jazz*
19 Knickerbocker ♪ 228-8490 — 33 University Pl *Jazz, Dining*
20 Bottom Line ♪ ✿ 228-7880 — 15 W. 4 *Folk, Rock*
21 Temple Bar ✔ 925-4242 — 332 Lafayette *Bar*
22 Great Jones Cafe 674-9304 — 54 Great Jones *Tex/Mex Bar*
23 CBGB ♪ 982-4052 — 315 Bowery *Hard Rock*
24 Dan Lynch ♪ 677-0911 — 221 Second Ave *Rock/Blues*

**🛍**
1 Pink Pussycat 243-0077 — 161 W. 4 *Erotica*
2 Balducci's ✿ 673-2600 — 424 Sixth Ave *Gourmet Food*
3 Bleeker Bob's 475-9677 — 118 W. 3 *Old Records*
4 Reminiscence 243-2292 — 74 Fifth Ave *Clothing*
5 Forbidden Planet 473-1576 — 821 Broadway *Sci-Fi*
6 Strand Books ✿ 473-1452 — 828 Broadway *Used Books*
7 Modern Age 674-5603 — 795 Broadway *Avant-Garde Furn*
8 Star Magic 228-7770 — 743 Broadway *Cosmic Gifts*
9 Unique ⊕ 674-1764 — 718 Broadway *Clothing*
10 Shakespeare & Co. 529-1330 — 716 Broadway *Books*
11 Tower Records ✿ 505-1500 — 692 Broadway *CDs, Records*

**⛪**
2 Grace Church 1864 — 800 Broadway *Renwick, Jr.*
3 Cooper Union 1859 — Cooper Square *Peterson*

**🖼**
1 Forbes Galleries 620-2389 — 62 Fifth Ave *Americana*

**🎭**
1 Cherry Lane — 38 Commerce, 989-2020
2 Charles Ludlam — 1 Sheridan Square, 691-2271
3 Minetta Lane — 18 Minetta Lane, 420-8000
4 Provincetown — 133 MacDougal, 477-5048
5 Sullivan Street — 181 Sullivan, 674-3838
6 Circle in the Square — 159 Bleeker, 254-6330
7 Public — 425 Lafayette, 598-7150
8 CSC Rep — 136 E. 13, 677-4210
9 Bouwerie Lane — 330 Bowery, 677-0060
10 La Mama — 74 E. 4 475-7710

**🏛**
1 Washington Sq. Arch ✿ 1876 — Washington Square *McKim et al*

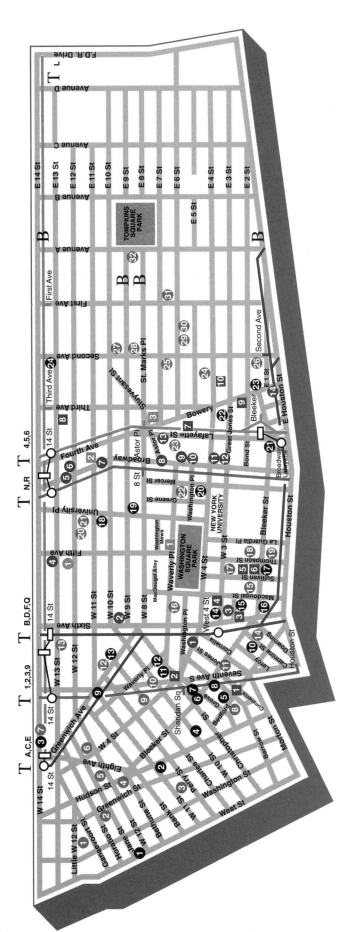

## 🍴

1 **Chelsea Central** *Am* $$$
227 Tenth Ave, 620-0230

2 **Empire Diner** *Am* $ ⌣
210 Tenth Ave, 243-2736

3 **La Luncheonette** *Fr* $$ X
130 Tenth Ave, 675-0342

4 **Frank's** *Am* $$$
431 W. 14, 243-1349

5 **Man Ray** *Fr* $$ ♈
169 Eighth Ave, 627-4220

6 **Miss Ruby's Cafe** *Cj* $$
135 Eighth Ave, 620-4055

7 **Chelsea Trattoria** *It* $$$
108 Eighth Ave, 924-7786

8 **Eze** *Fr* $$$ ✪
254 W. 23, 691-1140

9 **Le Madri** *It* $$$$ ✪ ⌣
168 W. 18, 727-8022

10 **Ozek** *Ja* $$
158 W. 23, 620-9131

11 **Da Umberto** *It* $$$
107 W. 17, 989-0303

12 **L'Acajou** *Fr* $$$
53 W. 19, 645-1706

13 **Periyali** *Gr* $$$
35 W. 20, 463-7890

14 **Lola** *Fr/Cb* $$$ ✪ ⌣ ♈ ♪
30 W. 22, 675-6700

15 **Eisenberg's** *Am* ⌣ 🅿
174 Fifth Ave, 675-5096

16 **Espace** *Fr* $$$
9 E. 16, 673-7676

17 **America** *Am* $ ✪ ♈
9 E. 18, 505-2110

18 **Union Sq. Cafe** *Am* $$$ ✪ ⌣
21 E. 16, 243-4020

19 **Cafe Galette** *Fr* $$$
23 E. 22, 353-9864

20 **Les Poulets** *Fr BBQ* ⌣ ⊕
27 E. 21, 254-5330

21 **Coffee Shop** *Bz* $$ ⌣ ♈
29 Union Sq W... 243-7969

22 **L'Escale** *Fr* $$
43 E. 20, 477-1180

23 **Positano** *It* $$$ ✪
250 Park Ave S., 777-6211

24 **Canastel's** *It* $$$ ⌣
229 Park Ave S., 677-9622

25 **Umeda** *Ja* $$
102 E. 22, 505-1550

26 **Lum Chin** *Ch* $
113 E. 18, 982-4485

27 **Maurya** *In* $$
129 East 27, 689-7925

28 **La Petite Auberge** *Fr* $$$
116 Lexington Ave, 689-5003

29 **Moreno** *It* $$$ ⌣
65 Irving Pl, 673-3939

30 **Sal Anthony's** *It* $$$
55 Irving Pl, 982-9030

31 **Sido Abu Salim** *ME* $$ ⊕
81 Lexington Ave, 686-2031

32 **Pete's Tavern** *Am* $ ✪ ♈
129 E. 18, 473-7676

33 **La Colombe d'Or** *Fr* $$$
134 E. 26, 689-0666

34 **Tatany** *Ja* $$
388 Third Ave, 686-1871

35 **Papa Bear** *Po* ⌣ X ⊕
210 E. 23, 685-0727

36 **Evita Argentine** *Ag* $$$
241 E. 24, 689-3783

37 **Health Pub** *Am* $
371 Second Ave, 529-9200

## 📷

1 **Citykids** 620-0906
130 Seventh Ave *Kids' Clothing*

2 **Barney's** ✪ 929-9000
111 Seventh Ave *Clothing*

3 **Jensen-Lewis** 929-4880
89 Seventh Ave *Furniture*

4 **Ace Banner & Flag** 620-9111
107 W. 27 *Custom Flags*

5 **Annex Flea Market** $$$
Sixth Ave/24-26 St, Sat/Sun

6 **Magickal Childe** 242-7182
35 W. 19 *Warlock Shop*

7 **Matsuda** 645-5151
156 Fifth Ave *W Clothing*

8 **Emporio Armani** 727-3240
110 Fifth Ave *Clothing*

9 **Paul Smith** 627-9770
108 Fifth Ave *M Clothing*

10 **Alain Mikli** 633-0777
100 Fifth Ave *Designer Eyeware*

11 **Dot Zero** 533-8322
159 Fifth Ave *Designware*

12 **Daffy's** ✂ 529-4477
111 Fifth Ave *Clothing*

13 **Barnes & Noble** 807-0099
105 Fifth Ave *Books, Texts*

14 **Gordon Novelty** 254-8616
933 Broadway *Masks/Novelties*

15 **Just Bulbs** 228-7820
938 Broadway *Lightbulbs*

16 **Design Letters** 673-6211
15 E.18 *Cut-out Letters*

17 **Hansen, Ken** 777-5900
920 Broadway *Pro. Cameras*

18 **See** 228-3600
920 Broadway *Italian Furn.*

19 **Fishs Eddy** 420-9020
889 Broadway *Used China*

20 **Last Wound-Up** 529-4197
889 Broadway *Wind-up Toys*

21 **Paragon** ✪ 255-8036
867 Broadway *Sporting Goods*

22 **ABC Carpet** 677-6970
888 Broadway *Carpets, Antiques*

23 **Swann Galleries** 254-4710
104 E. 25 *Auction House*

## 🌙

1 **Eagle Tavern** ♪ 924-0275
335 W. 14 *Traditional Irish*

2 **Delta 88** ♪ 924-3499
332 Eighth Ave *Jazz/Blues*

3 **Angry Squire** ♪ 242-9066
216 Seventh Ave *Jazz*

4 **Chelsea Billiards** 989-0096
54 W. 21 *Pool Hall*

5 **Tramps** ♪ 727-7788
45 W. 21 *Jazz/Blues*

6 **Chevy's** ♪ 924-0205
27 W. 20 *Rock/Dancing*

7 **Cadillac Bar** 645-7220
15 W. 21 *Bar*

8 **Cafe Society** ♪ 529-8282
915 Broadway *Cabaret, Dancing*

9 **M.K.** ⌣ ♪ 779-1340
204 Fifth Ave, *Dine, Dance*

10 **Live Bait** ⌣ 353-2400
14 E. 23 *Bar*

11 **Old Town Bar** 529-6732
45 E. 18 *Bar*

12 **Cafe Iguana** 529-4770
235 Park Ave S. *Bar*

13 **Condon's** ♪ 254-0960
117 E. 15 *Jazz*

14 **Caliban** ♪ 689-5155
360 Third Ave *Jazz, Dining*

15 **Fat Tuesday's** ♪ 533-7902
190 Third Ave *Jazz*

## 🏛

1 **Chelsea Hotel** 1884
222 W. 23 *Hubert, Pirsson*

2 **Flatiron Building** ✪ 1902
Fifth Ave/23 St *Burnham*

3 **Metropolitan Life** 1909
Madison Ave/23 -25 St *LeBrun*

4 **T. Roosevelt Birthplace** 1848
28 E. 20 *Riddle*

## 💃

1 **Kitchen, The** *Dance*
512 W. 19, 255-5793

2 **Chelsea Stage**
441 W.26, 645-4940

3 **Apple Corps**
336 W. 20, 627-3624

4 **Joyce Theater** *Dance*
175 Eighth Ave, 242-0800

5 **Dance Theater Workshop** *Dance*
219 W. 19, 924-0077

6 **Roundabout**
100 E. 17, 420-1883

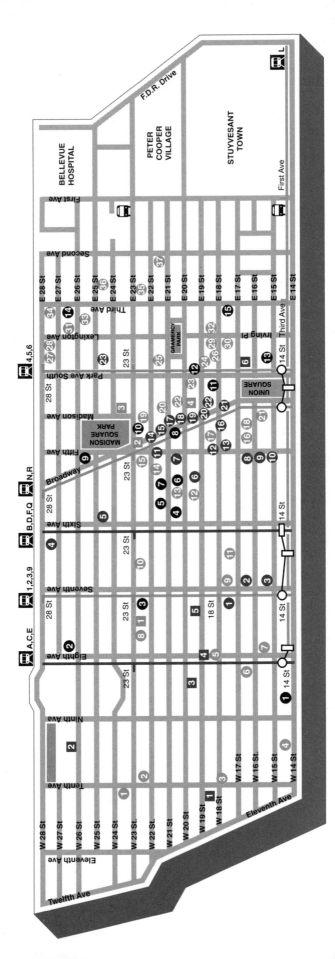

### 🍴

1 **Supreme Macaroni** *It* $$ X
511 Ninth Ave, 564-8074
2 **Bellevues** *Fr* $$ X ✔
496 Ninth Ave, 967-7850
3 **Manganaro's Hero-Boy** *It* X
492 Ninth Ave, 947-7325
4 **T.S. Ma** *Ch* $$
5 Penn Plaza, 971-0050
5 **Veronica Ristorante** *It* ( X
240 W. 38, 764-4770
6 **Chinese/American** *Ch* ( X ⊕
106 W. 32, 564-4597
7 **Keen's Chop House** *Am ST* $$$
72 W. 36, 947-3636
8 **Grappino** *It* $$
38 W. 39, 398-0350
9 **Lavin's** *Cont* $$
23 W. 39, 921-1288
10 **Sunny East** *Ch* $$
21 W. 39, 764-3232
11 **Genroku Sushi** *Ja* $$
366 Fifth Ave, 947-7940
12 **Fino** *It* $$
4 E. 36, 689-8040

13 **Young Bin Kwan** *Ko* $$
10 E. 38, 683-9031
14 **Bienvenue** *Fr* $$
21 E. 36, 684-0215
15 **Chez Laurence** *Fr* X (
245 Madison Ave, 683-0284
16 **Salta In Bocca** *It* $$
179 Madison Ave, 684-1757
17 **Samraat** *In* $$
175 Madison Ave, 213-1377
18 **Tempo** *It* $$
30 E. 29, 532-8125
19 **Cedars of Lebanon** *ME* $$
39 E. 30, 725-9251
20 **Hakubai** *Ja* $$$
66 Park Ave, 686-3770
21 **American Place, An** *Am* $$$
2 Park Ave, 684-2122
22 **Park Bistro** *Fr* $$
414 Park Ave S., 689-1360
23 **CI Ristorante** *It* $$ ♫
101 Park Ave, 972-0101
24 **Russell's** *Am* $$$
100 E. 37, 685-7676
25 **Time & Again** *Am/Fr* $$$ ⊕
116 E. 39, 685-8887

26 **Maison Japonaise** *Ja/Fr* $$
125 E. 39, 682-7375
27 **Stella del Mare** *It* $$$
346 Lexington Ave, 687-4425
28 **Sonia Rose** *Ec* $$
132 Lexington Ave, 545-1777
29 **Dolphin** *Am SF* $$$
227 Lexington Ave, 689-3010
30 **Curry-in-a-Hurry** *In* ( X ⊕
130 E. 29, 889-1159
31 **Courtyard Cafe** *It/Am* $$
130 E. 39, 779-0739
32 **Back Porch** *Am* $$
488 Third Ave, 685-3828
33 **Tibetan Kitchen** *Ti* $ X ⊕
444 Third Ave, 679-6286
34 **Sumptuary** *It/Fr* $$
400 Third Ave, 889-6056
35 **Dock's Oyster Bar** *Am* $$$
633 Third Ave, 986-8080
36 **Sakura Japan** *Ja* $$
581 Third Ave, 972-8540
37 **Jackson Hole** *Am* (
521 Third Ave, 679-3264
38 **Siu Lam Kung** *Ch* $ ⊕
499 Third Ave, 696-9099

39 **Pasticcio** *It* $$ 🅿
447 Third Ave, 679-2551
40 **Nicola Paone** *It* $$$
207 E. 34, 889-3239
41 **Marchi's** *It* $$$
251 E. 31, 679-2494
42 **Caterina** *It* $$ 🅿
720 Second Ave, 684-9559
43 **El Parador Cafe** *Mx* $$
325 E. 34, 679-6812
44 **Water Club, The** *Am* $$$$ ⊕
500 E. 30, 683-3333

### 🛍

1 **Executive Photo** ✆ 564-3592
120 W. 31 *Photo, Electronics*
2 **Macy's** ✪ 695-4400
151 W. 34 *Department Store*
3 **A&S** 594-8500
899 Sixth Ave *Department Store*
4 **Staples** ✆ 944-6744
1075 Sixth Ave *Office Supplies*
5 **Hyman Hendler** 840-8393
67 W. 38 *Ribbons*
6 **Sheru** 730-0766
49 W. 38 *Beads*

7 **Lord & Taylor** 391-3344
424 Fifth Ave *Department Store*
8 **Tannen's Magic** 239-8383
6 W. 32 *Magic Supplies*
9 **Sokolin, D.** 532-5893
178 Madison Ave *Wines/Spirits*
10 **Complete Traveller** 679-4339
199 Madison Ave *Travel Books*
11 **E-33** ℅ 686-0930
42 E. 33 *Electronics*
12 **Quark** 889-1808
537 Third Ave *Hi-Tech Electron.*
13 **Simon's Hardware** 532-9220
421 Third Ave *Decorative Hdwr.*

### 🏛

1 **Javits Convention Ctr.** ✪ 1986
Eleventh Ave/34-39 St *Pei*
1 **General Post Office** 1913
Eighth Ave/33 St *McKim et al*
2 **Madison Sq. Garden** 1968
Seventh Ave/33 St *Luckman*
3 **Pennsylvania Station**
Seventh Ave/33 St
4 **Empire State Building** ✪ 1931
350 Fifth Ave *Shreve et al*
5 **Marble Collegiate Church** 1854
272 Fifth Ave *Warner*
6 **Church/Transfiguration** 1849
1 E. 29

### 🏛

1 **Guinness Records Hall** 947-2339
350 Fifth Ave *Exhibits*
2 **Morgan Library** ✪ 685-0008
29 E. 36 *Art Museum*

### ♪

1 **Ballroom** ♫ 244-3005
253 W. 28 *Cabaret, Dining*
2 **41st Precinct** 679-3565
24 E. 41 *Bar*
3 **El Rio Grande** 867-0922
160 E. 38 *Bar, Dining*
4 **Zanzibar & Grill** ♫ 779-0606
550 Third Ave *Jazz*
5 **Wonderland** ♫ 213-5098
519 Second Ave *Blues, Dining*

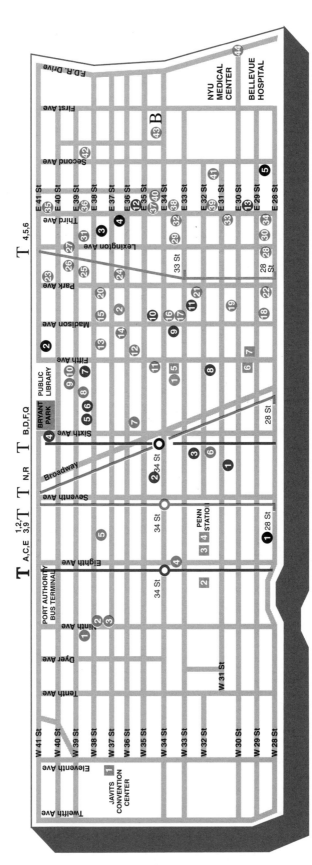

**🍴**

1 Mike's Amer. Bar *Am Mx* $ 📍 650 Tenth Ave, 246-4115
2 Le Madeleine *Fr* $$ 403 W. 43, 246-2993
3 Jezebel *Am* $$$ 630 Ninth Ave, 582-1045
4 Le Rivage *Fr* $$ 340 W. 46, 765-7374
5 Carolina *Am* $$$ 355 W. 46, 245-0058
6 Orso *It* $$$ 322 W. 46, 489-7212
7 Trixie's *Am Ec* $$ ♫ 307 W. 47, 840-9537
8 La Rivista *It* $$ 313 W. 46, 245-1707
9 B. Smith's *Am* $$$ ▮ ♫ 771 Eighth Ave, 247-2222
10 Pierre au Tunnel *Fr* $$$ 250 W. 47, 582-2166
11 Cabana Carioca *Bz* $ ⊕ 123 W. 45, 581-8088
12 Cafe Un Deux Trois *Fr* $$ 123 W. 44, 354-4148
13 Rainbow Room *Cont* $$$$ ✪ 🌟 30 Rockefeller Plaza, 632-5100
14 Sea Grill, The *Am SF* $$$$ ✪ 19 W. 49, 246-9201

19 Chikubu *Ja* $$$ 12 E. 44, 818-0715
20 Giambelli *It* $$$$ 46 E. 50, 688-2760
21 Take-Sushi *Ja X* $$$ 71 Vanderbilt Ave, 867-5120
22 Oyster Bar *Am SF* $$$ ✪ Grand Central Sta., 490-6650
23 Inagiku *Ja* $$$ ✪ 301 Park Ave, 355-0440
24 Tropica Bar/Seafood *SF* $$$ 200 Park Ave, 867-6767
25 J. Sung Dynasty *Ch* ✪ 511 Lexington Ave, 355-1200
26 Bukhara *In* $$$ 148 E. 48, 838-1811
27 Nanni's *It* $$$ 146 E. 46, 697-4161
28 Christ Cella *Am ST* $$$$ 160 E. 46, 697-2479
29 Smith & Wollensky *Am ST* $$$$ 201 E. 49, 753-1530
30 Fortune Garden *Ch* $$$ 209 E. 49, 753 0101
31 Chin Chin *Ch* $$$ 216 E. 49, 888-4555
32 Box Tree *Cont* $$$$ ⊕ 250 E. 49, 758-8320
33 Sparks Steak House *Am ST* $$$$ 210 E. 46, 687-4855

38 Palm, The *Am ST* $$$$ 837 Second Ave, 687-2953
39 Sichuan Pavilion *Ch* $$$ 310 E. 44, 972-7377
40 Ambassador Grill *Fr* $$$ ⊕ First Ave/44 St, 702-5014

**🎵**

2 Improvisation 765-8268 358 W. 44 *Comedy Club*
3 Danny's ♫ 265-8133 346 W. 46 *Piano Bar*
4 Don't Tell Mama ♫ 757-0788 343 W. 46 *Cabaret, Bar*
5 Indigo Blues ♫ 221-0033 221 W. 46 *Blues, Cabaret*
6 Rainbow/Stars 🌟 ♫ 632-5000 30 Rockefeller Plaza *Cabaret*
7 Jan Wallman's ♫ 764-8930 49 W. 44 *Cabaret*
8 Beekman Tower 🌟 ♫ 355-7300 First Av/49 St. *Piano Bar*

**🛍**

1 TKTS % 354-5800 Broadway/47 St *Theater Tickets*
2 Sam Ash 719-2299 155 W. 48 *Musical Instruments*
3 Hotalings News Depot 840-1868 142 W. 42 *Foreign/Domestic*
4 47th St. Photo % 260-4410 67 W. 47 *Cameras/Electronics*
5 Harvey Electronics 575-5000 2 W. 45 *Audio Equipment*
6 Saks Fifth Avenue ✪ 753-4000 611 Fifth Ave *Department Store*
7 Press, J. 687-7642 16 E. 44 *M Clothing*
8 Crouch & Fitzgerald 755-5888 400 Madison Ave *Luggage*
9 Tripler, F.R., 922-1090 366 Madison Ave *M Clothing*
10 Paul Stuart 682-0320 Madison/45 *M Clothing*
11 Brooks Bros. ✪ 682-8800 346 Madison Ave *M. Clothing*

**📷**

2 Int'l. Ctr. Photog. 768-4680 1133 Sixth Ave *Photography*
3 Whitney/Philip Morris 878-2550 120 Park Ave *Art*

**🏛**

1 Kaufman 534 W. 42, 564-8038
2 John Houseman 450 W. 42, 564-8038
3 Douglas Fairbanks 432 W. 42, 230-4321
4 South Street 424 W. 42, 279-4200
5 Playwrights Horizons 416 W. 42, 279-4200
6 Harold Clurman 412 W. 42, 695-3401
7 West Side Arts 407 W. 43, 541-8394
8 Martin Beck 302 W. 45, 246-0102
9 Ambassador 219 W. 49, 239-6200
10 Eugene O'Neill 230 W. 49, 246-0220
11 Longacre 220 W. 48, 239-6200
12 Barrymore 243 W. 47, 239-6200

**📷**

1 Circle Line ✪ 563-3200 Hudson River/42 St,
2 Times Square ✪ Broadway/42-50 St
3 Rockefeller Center ✪ 1931-40 Fifth Ave/48-50 St *Hood et al*
4 N.Y. Yacht Club 1899 37 W. 44 *Warren & Wetmore*
5 N.Y. Public Library 1911 Fifth Ave/42 St *Carrere & Hastings*
6 Grand Central Term. 1913 Park Ave/42 St *Reed & Stem*
7 Chrysler Building ✪ 1930 405 Lexington Ave *Van Alen*

17 Music Box 239 W. 45, 239-6200
18 Marquis 1535 Broadway, 382-0100
19 Golden 252 W. 45, 239-6200
20 Royale 242 W. 45, 239-6200
21 Plymouth 236 W. 45, 239-6200
22 Booth 222 W. 45, 239-6200
23 Minskoff 200 W. 45, 246-0102
24 Majestic 247 W. 44, 239-6200
25 Broadhurst 235 W. 44, 239-6200
26 Shubert 225 W. 44, 239-6200
27 St. James 246 W. 44, 246-0102
28 Helen Hayes 240 E. 44, 944-9450
29 Cort 138 W. 48, 239 6200
30 Palace 1564 Broadway, 730-8200
31 American Place 111 W. 46, 840-3074

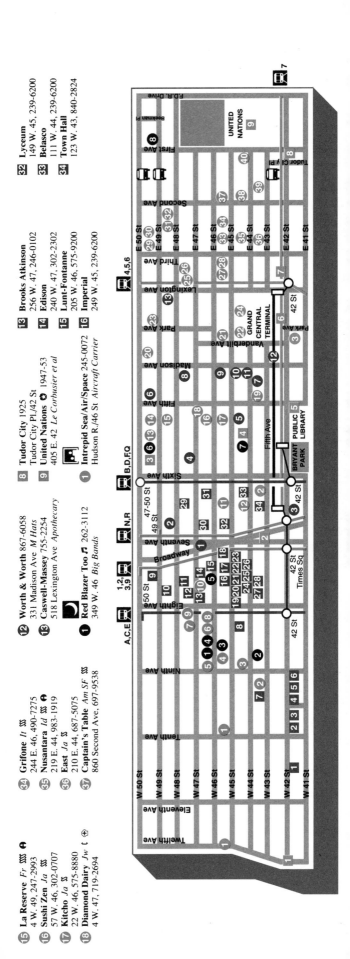

**15** La Reserve *Fr* $$$ 🔆
4 W. 49, 247-2993

**16** Sushi Zen *Ja* $$$
57 W. 46, 302-0707

**17** Kitcho *Ja* $$
22 W. 46, 575-8880

**18** Diamond Dairy *Jw* ¢ ♿
4 W. 47, 719-2694

**34** Grifone *It* $$$ 🔆
244 E. 46, 490-7275

**35** Nusantara *Id* $$$ 🔆
219 E. 44, 983-1919

**36** East *Ja* $$
210 E. 44, 687-5075

**37** Captain's Table *Am SF* $$$
860 Second Ave, 697-9538

**12** Worth & Worth 867-6058
331 Madison Ave *M* Hats

**13** Caswell-Massey 755-2254
518 Lexington Ave *Apothecary*

**1** Red Blazer Too ♪ 262-3112
349 W. 46 *Big Bands*

**8** Brooks Atkinson
256 W. 47, 246-0102

**14** Edison
240 W. 47, 302-2302

**15** Lunt-Fontanne
205 W. 46, 575-9200

**16** Imperial
249 W. 45, 239-6200

**32** Lyceum
149 W. 45, 239-6200

**33** Belasco
111 W. 44, 239-6200

**34** Town Hall
123 W. 43, 840-2824

**8** Tudor City 1925
Tudor City Pl/42 St

**9** United Nations ✪ 1947-53
405 E. 42 *Le Corbusier et al*

**1** Intrepid Sea/Air/Space 245-0072
Hudson R./46 St *Aircraft Carrier*

## Restaurants

1. Afghan Kebab *Af* $ ⊕ — 764 Ninth Ave., 307-1612
2. Bangkok Cuisine *Th* $$ — 885 Eighth Ave., 581—6370
3. Siam Inn *Th* $$ ⊕ — 916 Eighth Ave., 489-5237
4. Hard Rock Cafe *Am* $ — 221 W. 57, 459-9320
5. Broadway Diner *Am* $ X — 1726 Broadway, 765-0909
6. Carnegie Deli *Jw~* $ X ⊕ ⊕ — 854 Seventh Ave., 757-2245
7. Petrossian *Ru* ⊕ — 182 W. 58, 245-2214
8. Russian Tea Room *Ru* $$$ ⊕ ✪ — 150 W. 57, 265-0947
9. Le Bernardin *Fr SF* $$$$ ⊕ — 155 W. 51, 489-1515
10. Remi *It* $$$ ⊕ ⊌ — 145 W. 53
11. Manhattan Ocean *Am SF* $$$ ⊕ — 57 W. 58, 371-7777
12. Marie-Michelle *It* $$$ — 57 W. 56, 315-2444
13. La Bonne Soupe *Fr* $ ⊕ — 48 W. 55, 586-7650
14. Darbar *In* $$$ — 44 W. 56, 432-7227
18. La Grenouille *Fr* $$$$ ⊕ ⊌ — 3 E. 52, 752-1495
19. Shinwa *Ja* $$ — 645 Fifth Ave., 644-7400
20. Quilted Giraffe *Ja Fr* $$$$ ⊕ — 550 Madison Ave., 593-1221
21. Le Cygne *Fr* $$$ ⊕ — 55 E. 54, 759-5941
22. Mitsukoshi *Ja* $$$ ⊕ — 461 Park Ave, 935-6444
23. Four Seasons *Am/Fr* $$$$ ⊕ ⊌ ✪ — 99 E. 52, 754-9494
24. Shun Lee Palace *Ch* $$$ ⊕ ✪ — 155 E. 55, 371-8844
25. Les Tournebroches *Fr* $$ — 153 E. 53, 935 6029
26. Nippon *Ja* $$ — 155 E. 52, 355-9020
27. Contrapunto *It* $$ — 200 E. 60, 751-8616
28. Arizona *Am* $$$ — 206 E. 60, 838-0440
29. Tre Scalini *It* $$$ — 230 E. 58, 688-6888
30. Clarke's, P.J. *Am* $$ ⊕ — 915 Third Ave., 759-1650
31. Toscana *It* $$$ ⊕ — 200 E. 54, 371-8144
32. Il Nido *It* $$$$ — 251 E. 53, 753-8450
36. Chez Louis *Fr* $$$ — 1016 Second Ave, 752-1400
37. Rosa Mexicano *Mx* $$$ — 1063 First Ave., 753-7407
38. Le Perigord *Fr* $$$$ — 405 E. 52, 755-6244
39. Wylie's Ribs *Am BBQ* $ ⊕ — 891 First Ave, 751-0700

## Shops

1. Rizzoli 759-2424 — 31 W. 57 *Books. Art. Foreign*
2. Bennis/Edwards 755-4192 — 22 W. 57 *Shoes*
3. Bendel, Henri 247-1100 — 10 W. 57 *W Clothing*
4. M.O.M.A. Design 708-9700 — 44 W. 53 *Designware*
5. Bergdorf Goodman 753-7300 — 754 Fifth Ave *Clothing*
6. Traveler's Bookstore 664-0995 — 22 W. 52 *Travel Books*
7. F.A.O. Schwarz ✪ 644-9400 — 767 Fifth Ave *Toys*
8. Chanel 355-5050 — 5 East 57 *W Clothing. Access.*
9. Tiffany ✪ 755-8000 — 727 Fifth Ave *Jewelry. Silverware*
10. Trump Tower — 725 Fifth Ave *Upscale Boutiques*
14. Christie's 546 1000 — 502 Park Ave *Auction House*
15. Anthony, T. 750-9797 — 480 Park Ave *Luggage*
16. Palazzetti 832-1199 — 515 Madison Ave. *Modern Furn.*
17. Argosy Books ⊕ 753-4455 — 116 E. 59 *Old Books, Prints*
18. Place des Antiquaires 758-2900 — 125 E. 57 *Antique Shops*
19. Bloomingdale's ✪ 355-5900 — 1000 Third Ave *Department Store*
20. Hammacher Schlemmer 421-9000 — 147 E. 57 *Gadgets*
21. Nassau, Lillian 759-6062 — 220 E. 57 *Ant. Tiffany Glass*
22. Bridge Kitchenware 688-4220 — 214 E. 52 *Professional Supplies*
23. Manhat. Antique Ctr. 355-4400 — 1050 Second Ave *Antique Shops*
24. Wim & Karen 758-4207 — 319 E. 53 *Scandinavian Furniture*

## Nightlife

1. Ritz ♫ 541-8900 — 254 W. 54 *Rock. Dancing*
2. Lone Star Roadhouse ♫ 245-2950 — 240 W. 52 *Country. Rock*
3. Edwardian Room ⊕ 759-3000 — Fifth Av/59 St *Dining. Dancing*

## Landmarks

1. Carnegie Hall 1891 — Seventh Ave/57 St *Tuthill et al*
2. Plaza Hotel 1907 — Fifth Ave/59 St
3. CBS Headquarters 1965 — 51 W. 52 *Saarinen*
4. Radio City Music Hall 1932 — Sixth Ave/50 St *Hood et al*
5. St. Thomas Church 1914 — Fifth Ave/53 St *Cram, Goodhue*
6. Paley Park 1967 — 3 E. 53 *Zion & Breen*
7. St. Patrick's Cathedral 1879 — Fifth Ave/50 St *Renwick*
8. Villard Houses 1884 — 451 Madison Ave *McKim et al*
9. Lever House 1952 — Park Ave/53 St *Skidmore et al*
10. Seagram Building ✪ 1958 — 375 Park Ave *Van Der Rohe*
11. Roosevelt Island Tram 1976 — Second Ave/59 St

## Museums & Galleries

6. Hammer 644-4405 — 33 W. 57 *19th- 20th-Cent. Art*
7. Mus. of Modern Art ✪ 708-9400 — 11 W. 53 *20th-Century Art*
8. American Craft Mus. 956-6047 — 40 W. 53 *Contemporary Crafts*
9. Mus. of Broadcasting 752-7684 — 1 East 53 *Radio and Television*
10. I.B.M. Gallery 407-6100 — 590 Madison *Science and Art*
11. A.C.A. 644-8300 — 41 E. 57 *20th-Century Art*
12. Emmerich, Andre 752-0124 — 41 E. 57 *Contemporary Art*
13. Pace 421-3292 — 32 East 57 *Contemp. Art, Prints*
1. Janis, Sidney 586-0110 — 110 W. 57 *Contemporary Art*
2. Frumkin/Adams 757-6655 — 50 W. 57 *Contemporary Art*

## Theaters

1. Virginia — 245 W. 52, 246-0102
2. Neil Simon — 250 W. 52, 757-8646
3. Uris — 222 W. 51, 586-6510
4. Mark Hellinger — 237 W. 51, 757-7064
5. Broadway — 1681 Broadway, 239-6200
6. Circle in the Square — 235 W. 50, 239-6200

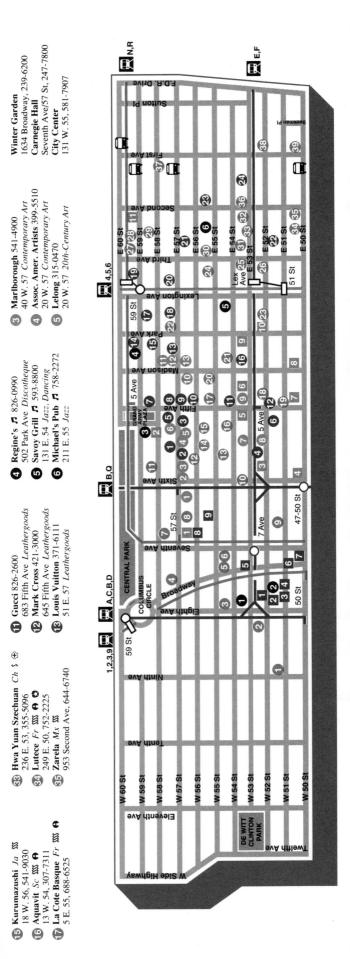

**15** Kurumazushi *Ja* $$$
18 W. 56, 541-9030
**16** Aquavit *Sc* $$$$
13 W. 54, 307-7311
**17** La Cote Basque *Fr* $$$$
5 E. 55, 688-6525

**33** Hwa Yuan Szechuan *Ch* $
236 E. 53, 355-5096
**34** Lutece *Fr* $$$$
249 E. 50, 752-2225
**35** Zarela *Mx* $$$
953 Second Ave, 644-6740

**3** Marlborough 541-4900
40 W. 57 *Contemporary Art*
**4** Assoc. Amer. Artists 399-5510
20 W. 57 *Contemporary Art*
**5** Lelong 315-0470
20 W. 57 *20th-Century Art*

**4** Regine's 826-0990
502 Park Ave *Discotheque*
**5** Savoy Grill 593-8800
131 E. 54 *Jazz, Dancing*
**6** Michael's Pub 758-2272
211 E. 55 *Jazz*

**11** Gucci 826-2600
683 Fifth Ave *Leathergoods*
**12** Mark Cross 421-3000
645 Fifth Ave *Leathergoods*
**13** Louis Vuitton 371-6111
51 E. 57 *Leathergoods*

**Winter Garden**
1634 Broadway, 239-6200
**Carnegie Hall**
Seventh Ave/57 St, 247-7800
**City Center**
131 W. 55, 581-7907

# NavigatorMap · 60th to 74th Street

## 🍴

1. **Cafe Luxembourg** *Fr* $$$ ✓
   200 W. 70, 873-7411
2. **Genoa** *It* $$
   271 Amsterdam Ave, 787-1094
3. **Fine & Schapiro** *Jw* $ 🅿
   138 W. 72, 877-2874
4. **Cafe Belcanto** *It* $$$
   1991 Broadway, 362-4642
5. **Andiamo** *It* $$$
   1991 Broadway, 362-3315
6. **Levana** *Ko* $$$
   141 W. 69, 877-8457
7. **Victor's** *Cu* $$
   240 Columbus Ave, 595-8599
8. **Lenge** *Ja* $$
   200 Columbus Av, 799-9188
9. **Cameos** *Am* $$$
   169 Columbus Ave, 874-2280
10. **La Boite en Bois** *Fr* $$$ X
    75 W. 68, 874-2705
11. **Dallas B.B.Q.** *Am* $
    27 W. 72, 873-2004
12. **Settanta Due** *It* $$$
    20 W 72, 787-5656
13. **Sidewalker's** *Am SF* $$$
    12 W. 72, 799-6070
14. **Santa Fe** *Mx* $$$
    72 W. 69, 724-0822
15. **Shun Lee West** *Ch* $$$
    43 W. 65, 595-8895
16. **Ginger Man** *Am* $$$ ▼
    51 W. 64, 399-2358
17. **Punch** *Fr/Sc* ✓
    11 W. 60, 767-0606
18. **Cafe des Artistes** *Fr* $$$$ 🖐 ✪
    1 W. 67, 877-3500
19. **Tavern/Green** *Cont* $$$$ 🖐 ✪
    Central Park W./67 St, 873-3200
20. **Arcadia** *Am* $$$
    21 E. 62, 223-2900
21. **Le Regence** *Fr* $$$$ 🖐
    37 E. 64, 606-4647
22. **Post House** *Am* $$$$
    28 E. 63, 935-2888
23. **Capriccio** *It* $$$
    33 E. 61, 757-7795
24. **Aureole** *Fr/Am* $$$$ 🖐
    34 E. 61, 319-1660
25. **Le Cirque** *Fr* $$$$ 🖐 ✓ ✪
    58 E. 65, 794-9292
26. **Regency** *Fr* $$$$
    540 Park Ave, 759-4100
27. **Gino** *It* $$$
    780 Lexington Ave, 758-4466
28. **Sette Mezzo** *It* $$$ X 🖐
    969 Lexington Ave, 472-0400
29. **Sign of the Dove** *Fr/Am* $$$$ 🖐
    1110 Third Ave, 861-8080
30. **John Clancy's** *Am SF* $$$
    206 E. 63, 752-6666
31. **Fu's** *Ch* $$$
32. **Afghan Kebab** *Af* $
    1395 Second Ave, 517-9670
33. **Uskudak** *Tk* $$ 🖐
    1345 Second Ave, 517-2776
34. **Cafe Greco** *Med*
    1405 Second Ave, 988-2641
35. **Primola** *It* $$$ 🖐
    1226 Second Ave, 758-1775
36. **Tanjore** *In* $$
    1229 First Ave, 517-7578
37. **Auntie Yuan** *Ch* $$$ 🖐
    1191A First Ave, 744-4040
38. **Malaga** *Sp* $$ 🖐 🅿
    406 E. 73, 737-7659
39. **John's Pizzeria** *It* ℂ X ⊕ 🅿
    408 E. 64, 935-2895

## 🎵

1. **Mrs. J's Sacred Cow** ♫ 873-4067
   *Piano Bar* — 228 W. 72
2. **Sweetwater's** ♫ 873-4100
   *Cabaret* — 170 Amsterdam Ave
3. **Steve McGraw's** ♫ 595-7400
   *Cabaret* — 158 W. 72
4. **Baja** 724-8890
5. **Polo Lounge** ♫ 535-2000
   *Dance Club* — 246 Columbus Ave
6. **Adam's Apple** ♫ 371-8651
   *Pop/Rock Dance* — 1117 First Ave
7. **Dangerfield's** 593-1650
   *Comedy* — 1118 First Ave

## 🏛

1. **Ansonia Hotel** 1904
   2109 Broadway *Graves & Duboy*
2. **Lincoln Center** ✪ 1962-68
   140 W. 65 *Harrison et al*
3. **Dakota Apartments** ✪ 1884
   1 W. 72 *Hardenbergh*
4. **Central Park Zoo**
   Fifth Ave/54 St (861-6030)
5. **Temple Emanu-El** 1929
   1 E. 65 *Kohn, Butler, Stein*

## 🛍

5. **Magazine Store** 397-3061
   1886 Broadway *Periodicals*
6. **Poster Originals** 861-0422
   924 Madison Ave *Art Posters*
7. **Missoni** 517-9339
   836 Madison Ave *Clothing*
8. **Porthault, D.** 686-1860
   18 E. 69 *Luxury Linens*
9. **Martin's, Billy** 861-3100
   812 Madison Ave *Western Wear*
10. **Ford, Rita** $$$ 🅿 535-6717
    19 E. 65 *Music Boxes*
11. **Polo/Ralph Lauren** ✪ 606-2100
    867 Madison Ave *Clothing*
12. **Armani, Giorgio** 988-9191
    815 Madison Ave *Clothing*
13. **Sherry-Lehmann** 838-7500
    679 Madison Ave *Wines, Spirits*
14. **Il Papiro** 288-9330
    1021 Lexington Ave *Paper Prod.*
15. **Tender Buttons** ✪ 758-7004
    143 E. 62 *New/Antique Buttons*
16. **Grace's Marketplace** 737-0600
    1237 Third Ave *Gourmet Food*
17. **Pedal Pusher** 288-5592
    1306 Second Ave *Bike Sales/Rental*
18. **Darrow's Antiques** 838-0730
    1164A Second Ave *Toys, Games*
19. **Antique/Flea Market**
    First Ave/67 St *Sat. 9-5*

## 🎵

1. **Tower Records** 799-2500
   1961 Broadway *CDs, Records*
2. **Last Wound-Up** 787 3388
   290 Columbus Ave *Wind-up Toys*
3. **Only Hearts** 724-5608
   281 Columbus Ave *Objets d'Heart*
4. **Charivari 72** 787-7272
   257 Columbus Ave *Clothing*

## 🏛

6. **Metropolitan Club** 1893
   1 E. 60 *Mckim, Mead, White*

## 🖼

1. **Mus./Amer. Folk Art** 595-9533
   2 Lincoln Sq. *Arts, Crafts*
2. **Frick Collection** ✪ 288-0700
   1 E. 70 *Old Masters*
3. **Knoedler & Co.** 794-0550
   19 E. 70 *Contemp. Eur/Amer Art*
4. **Hirschl & Adler** 535-8810
   21 E. 70 *Eur/Amer Art, Amer Folk*
5. **Wildenstein** 879-0500
   19 E. 64 *Masters, Modern Art*
6. **Didier Aaron** 988-5248
   32 E. 67 *Eur/Orient Art & Furn.*
7. **Center for African Art** 861-1200
   54 E. 68 *African Art*
8. **Asia Society** 288-6400
   725 Park Ave *Asian Arts*

## 🖼 (auction)

20. **Sotheby's** 606-7000
    1334 York Ave *Auction House*

## 🎭

**Lincoln Center** ✪
140 W. 65:
1. **Juilliard Theater** 874-7515
2. **Alice Tully Hall** 362-1911
3. **Vivian Beaumont** 239-6200
4. **Avery Fisher Hall** 874-2424
5. **Metropolitan Opera** 362-3000
6. **N.Y. State Theater** 870-5570

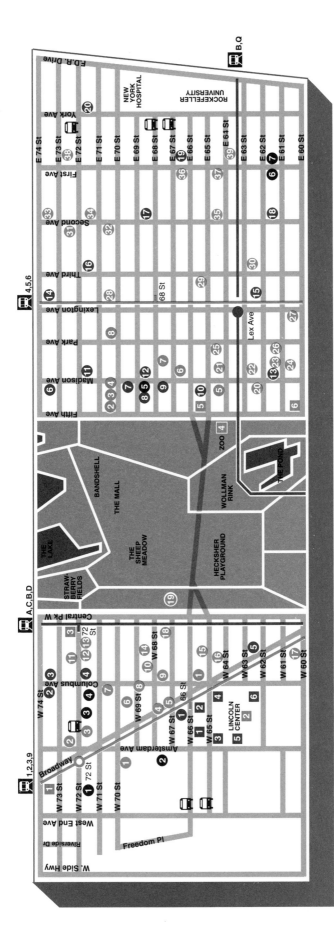

## 🍴

1 **La Mirabelle** *Fr* $$$ 333 W. 86, 496-0458
2 **Caffe Bernini** *It* $$ X ♥ 250 W. 77, 496-6674
3 **Boulevard** *Am* $$ 2398 Broadway, 874-7400
4 **Yellow Rose** *Mx* $ 450 Amsterdam Ave, 595-8760
5 **Amsterdam's** *Am* $$ ♥ 428 Amsterdam Ave, 874-1377
6 **Baci** *It* $$ X 412 Amsterdam Ave, 496-1550
7 **Au Rivage** *Cont.* $$$ 408 Amsterdam Ave, 787-6900
8 **Melon, J.G.** *Am* $ X ♥ 340 Amsterdam Ave, 874-8291
9 **Ernie's** *It* $$ 2150 Broadway, 496-1588
10 **Coastal** *Am* $$$ 300 Amsterdam Ave, 769-3988
11 **Popover Cafe** *Am* $ ♥ 551 Amsterdam Ave, 595-8555
12 **Good Enough to Eat** *Am* $$ 483 Amsterdam Ave, 496-0163
13 **Sarabeth's Kitchen** *Am* 423 Amsterdam Ave, 496-6280
14 **Alcala** *Sp* $$$ 349 Amsterdam Ave, 769-9600
15 **Bimini Twist** *Cb* $$ 345 Amsterdam Ave, 362-1260
16 **Nishi** *Ja* $$$ X ♥ 325 Amsterdam Ave, 799-0117
17 **Poiret** *Fr* $$$ ♥ 474 Columbus Ave, 724-6880
18 **Mughlai** *In* $$ 320 Columbus Ave, 724-6363
19 **Fujiyama Mama** *Ja* $$$ ♥ ♫ 467 Columbus Ave, 769-1144
20 **Isabella's** *It* $$ 359 Columbus Ave, 724-2100
21 **Memphis** *Cj* $$$ ♥ 329 Columbus Ave, 496-1840
22 **Kalinka** *Ru* $ 1067 Madison Ave, 472- 9656
23 **Le Refuge** *Fr* $$$ X ♥ 166 E. 82, 861-4505
24 **Sam's Cafe** *Am* ◡ ♈ 1406 Third Ave, 988-5300
25 **Jim McMullen** *Am* $$$ ♈ 1341 Third Ave, 861-4700
26 **Mezzaluna** *It* $$$ X ♈ 1295 Third Ave, 535-9600
27 **Natalino** *It* $$ ♥ 243 E. 78, 737-3771
28 **Vico** *It* $$ X 1603 Second Ave, 772-7441
29 **Csarda** *Hg* $$ 1477 Second Ave, 472-2892
30 **Pamir** *Af* $$ ♥ 1437 Second Ave, 734-3791
31 **Paola's** *It* $$$ ♥ 347 E. 85, 794-1890
32 **Mocca** *Hg* $$ X ♥ 1588 Second Ave, 734-6470
33 **Gijo's** *It* $$ 1574 Second Ave, 772-0752
34 **Istanbul Cuisine** *Tk* $ X ♥ 303 E. 80, 744-6903
35 **Quatorze Bis** *Fr* $$$ ♥ 323 E. 79, 535-1414
36 **Vasata** *Cz* $$$ ♥ 339 E. 75, 988-7166
37 **Via Ristorante** *It* $$$ ♥ 1489 First Ave, 517-4892
38 **Bangkok House** *Th* $$ ♥ 1485 First Ave, 249-5700
39 **Dieci** *It* $ X 1568 First Ave, 628-6565
40 **Voulez-Vous** *Fr* $$$ 1462 First Ave, 249-1776
41 **Szechuan Kitchen** *Ch* $ X ♈ 1460 First Ave, 249-4615
42 **Wilkinson's Seafood** *SF* $$$ 1573 York Ave, 535-5454
43 **City Cafe** *Am* $$ ♥ 1481 York Ave, 570-9810
44 **Tour de France** *Fr* $$ 1428 York Ave, 744-7844

## 🛍

1 **Charivari for Men** 873-7242 2339 Broadway *M Clothing*
2 **Shakespeare & Co.** 580-7800 2259 Broadway *Books*
3 **Zabar's** ♥ 787-2000 2245 Broadway *Gourmet Food*
4 **Eeyore's** 362-0634 2212 Broadway *Kids' Books*
5 **Alice Underground** 724-6682 380 Columbus Ave *Ant. Clothing*
6 **Mythology Unlimited** ♥ 874-0774 370 Columbus Ave *Eclectic Toys*
7 **I.S. 44 Flea Market** ♥ Columbus Ave/76-77 St *Sun. 10-6*
8 **Maxilla & Mandible** 724-6173 451 Columbus Ave *Skeletons*
9 **Soldier Shop** 535-6788 1222 Madison Ave *Antique Toys*
10 **Time Will Tell** 861-2663 962 Madison Ave *Antique Watches*
11 **Chocolate Soup** 861-2210 946 Madison Ave *Kids' Clothing*
12 **Stair & Co.** 517-4400 942 Madison Ave *Antique Furn.*
13 **Books & Co.** 737-1450 939 Madison Ave *Books*
14 **Jenny B. Goode** 794-2492 1194 Lexington Ave *Designware*
15 **Go Fly a Kite** 472-2623 1201 Lexington Ave *Kites*
16 **Doyle, William** 427-2730 175 E. 87 *Auction House*

## 🎵

1 **Stand-Up N.Y.** 595-0850 236 W. 78 *Comedy*
2 **China Club** ♫ 877-1166 2130 Broadwa *Rock/Dance*
3 **Raccoon Lodge** 874-9984 480 Amsterdam Ave *Bar*
4 **Cafe Carlyle** ♫ ♥ 744-1600 Madison Ave/76 St *Cabaret*
5 **Bemelman's Bar** ♫ 744-1600 35 E. 76 *Piano Bar*
6 **Wicked Wolf** 861-4670 1442 First Ave *Bar*
7 **Zulu Lounge** 772-0556 1584 York Ave *Dance*

## 🛏

1 **Beresford** 1929 211 Central Pk. W. *Roth*
2 **San Remo** 1930 145 Central Pk. W. *Roth*
3 **998 Fifth Avenue** 1910 998 Fifth Ave *McKim et al*
4 **Gracie Mansion** 1798 East End Ave/88 St *Schmidt*

## 🏛

1 **Am. Mus. Nat. Hist.** ♥ 769-5000 Central Pk. W./79 St, *Life on Earth*
2 **Hayden Planetarium** 873-8828 Central Pk. W./81 St *Astronomy*
3 **N.Y. Historical Soc.** 873-3400 Central Pk. W./77 St *Americana*
4 **Metropol. Mus. Art** ♥ 879-5500 Fifth Ave/82 St *Ancient/Cont. Art*
5 **Acquavella Galleries** 734-6300 18 E. 79 *20th-Century Art*
6 **Salander-O'Reilly** 879-6606 20 E. 79 *19th- 20th-Century Art*
7 **Graham** 535-5767 1014 Mad. Ave *20th-Cent. Art*
8 **Stone, Allen** 787-8533 48 E. 86 *Contemporary Art*
9 **Whitney Museum** ♥ 570-3676 Mad. Ave/75 St *Mod. Amer. Art*
10 **North of 88th St. (off map):**
**Cooper-Hewitt Mus.** 860-6868 Fifth Ave/91 St *Design/Decor.*
**Guggenheim Mus.** ♥ 360-3500 Fifth Ave/89 *Art (Reopens 10/91)*
**Jewish Museum** 860-1888 Fifth Ave/92 St *Judaica*
**Mus/City of N.Y.** 534-1672 Fifth Ave/103 St *NY History*

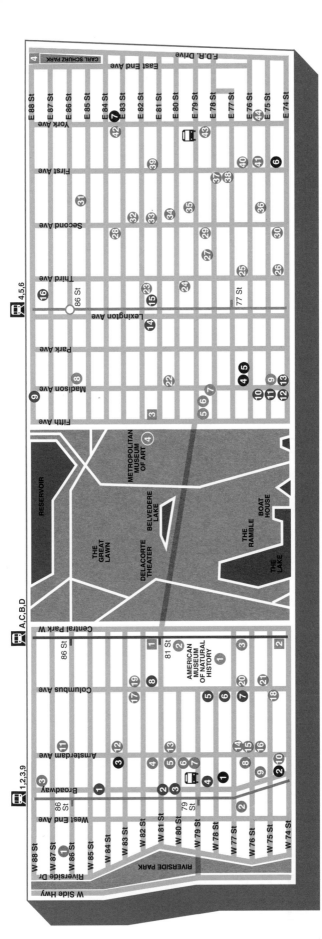

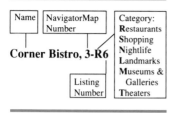

## INDEX

Name | NavigatorMap Number | Category:
**Corner Bistro, 3-R6**
Listing Number

Category: **R**estaurants **S**hopping **N**ightlife **L**andmarks **M**useums & Galleries **T**heaters

---

Restaurants   Shopping   Nightlife   Landmarks   Museums & Galleries   Theaters

Star Magic, 3-S8
Staten Island Ferry, 1-L12
Statue of Liberty (Ferry), 1-L6
Stella del Mare, 5-R27
Steve McGraw's, 8-N3
St. James Theater, 6-T27
Stone, Allen, Gallery, 9-M8
St. Patrick's Cathedral, 7-L7
St. Paul's Chapel, 1-L4
Strand Books, 3-S6
St. Thomas Church, 7-L5
Sullivan Street Theater, 3-T5
Sumptuary, 5-R34
Sunny East, 5-R10
Supreme Macaroni, 5-R1
Sushi Zen, 6-R16
Swann Galleries, 4-S23
Sweet Basil, 3-N8
Sweets, 1-R8
Sweetwater's, 8-N2
Syms, 1-S1
Szechuan Kitchen, 9-R41

**T**
Tai Hong Lau, 1-R33
Take-Sushi, 6-R21
Tanjore, 8-R36
Tannen's Magic, 5-S8
Taormina, 2-R22
Tatany, 4-R34
Tavern on the Green, 8-R19
Temple Bar, 3-N21
Temple Emanu-El, 8-L5
Tempo, 5-R18
Tender Buttons, 8-S15
Tennessee Mountain, 2-R13
Tents & Trails, 1-S5
Thai House Cafe, 1-R12
Thailand Restaurant, 1-R29
Theodore Roosevelt Birthplace, 4-L4
Think Big, 2-S7
Thunder & Light, 2-S28
Tibetan Kitchen, 5-R33
Tiffany, 7-S9
Time & Again, 5-R25
Times Square, 6-L2
Time Will Tell, 9-S10
TKTS, 6-S1
Tommy Tang's, 1-R15
Tompkins Park, 3-R32
Tootsi Plohound, 2-S13
Toscana, 7-R31
Tour de France, 9-R44
Tower Flea Market, 3-S12
Tower Records, 3-S11, 8-S1
Town Hall, 6-T34
Tramps, 4-N5
Traveler's Bookstore, 7-S6
Tre Scalini, 7-R29
Tribeca Grill, 1-R13
Trinity Church, 1-L5
Tripler, F.R., 6-S9
Trixie's, 6-R7
Tropica Bar/Seafood, 6-R24
Trump Tower, 7-S10

T.S. Ma, 5-R4
Tudor City, 6-L8
20 Mott Street, 1-R37

**U**
Umeda, 4-R25
Uncle Steve, 2-S18
Union Square Cafe, 4-R18
Unique, 3-S9
United Nations, 6-L9
Untitled, 2-S4
Urban Archeology, 2-S26
Uris Theater 7-T3
U.S. Customs House, 1-L9
Uskudak, 8-R33

**V**
Vasata, 9-R36
Veronica Ristorante, 5-R5
Veselka, 3-R28
Via Ristorante, 9-R37
Vico, 9-R28
Victor's, 8-R7
Village Gate, 3-N17
Village Vanguard, 3-N9
Villard Houses, 7-L8
Virginia Theater 7-T1
Vivian Beaumont Theater, 8-T3
Voulez-Vous, 9-R40
Vucciria, 2-R10

**W**
Washington Square Arch, 3-L1
Water Club, 5-R44
Weber Gallery, 2-M9
West Side Arts Theater, 6-T7
Wetlands, 1-N2
White Horse Tavern, 3-N2
Whitney Museum/Downtown, 1-M1
Whitney Museum of American Art,
   9-M9
Whitney Museum/Philip Morris,
   6-M3
Wicked Wolf, 9-N6
Wildenstein Gallery, 8-M5
Wilkinson's Seafood, 9-R42
Wim & Karen, 7-S24
Windows on the World, 1-R4
Winter Garden, 7-T7
Witkin Gallery, 2-M3
Wolfman Gold, 2-S19
Wonderland, 5-N5
Wonton Garden, 1-R34
Woolworth Building, 1-L15
World Financial Center, 1-L1
World Trade Center, 1-L3
Worth & Worth, 6-S12
Wylie's Ribs, 7-R39

**Y**
Yellow Rose, 9-R4
Young Bin Kwan, 5-R13

**Z**
Zabar's, 9-S3
Zanzibar & Grill, 5-N4
Zarela, 7-R35
Zona, 2-S17
Zulu Lounge, 9-N7

---

**NavigatorMap
number and
area covered:**

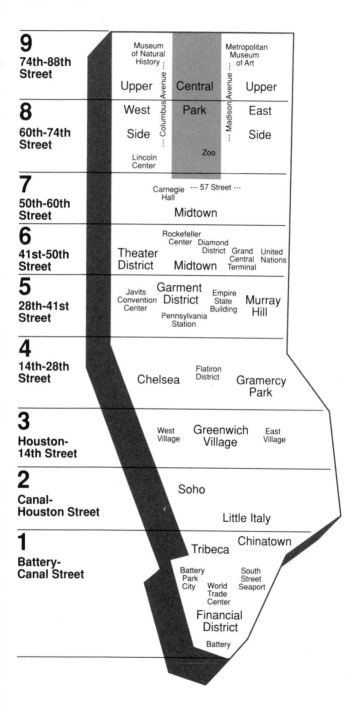

**9**
**74th-88th
Street**

**8**
**60th-74th
Street**

**7**
**50th-60th
Street**

**6**
**41st-50th
Street**

**5**
**28th-41st
Street**

**4**
**14th-28th
Street**

**3**
**Houston-
14th Street**

**2**
**Canal-
Houston Street**

**1**
**Battery-
Canal Street**

Museum of Natural History

Metropolitan Museum of Art

Upper West Side

Central Park

Upper East Side

Columbus Avenue

Madison Avenue

Lincoln Center

Zoo

Carnegie Hall --- 57 Street ---

Midtown

Rockefeller Center  Diamond District  Grand Central Terminal  United Nations

Theater District

Midtown

Garment District

Javits Convention Center

Empire State Building

Murray Hill

Pennsylvania Station

Chelsea

Flatiron District

Gramercy Park

West Village

Greenwich Village

East Village

Soho

Little Italy

Chinatown

Tribeca

Battery Park City

World Trade Center

South Street Seaport

Financial District

Battery